BLUE-COLLAR ARISTOCRATS

BLUE-COLLAR

ARISTOCRATS

Life-Styles at a Working-Class Tavern

E. E. LeMASTERS

HD
8072
.L37

The University of Wisconsin Press

Published 1975
The University of Wisconsin Press
Box 1379, Madison, Wisconsin 53701

The University of Wisconsin Press, Ltd.
70 Great Russell Street, London

First printing

Printed in the United States of America

ISBN 0-299-06550-2 (cloth), 0-299-06554-5 (paper)

Composed by the Composing Room, Grand Rapids, Michigan
Manufactured by George Banta Co., Inc., Menasha, Wisconsin
Designed by Gary Gore

Library of Congress Cataloging in Publication Data

LeMasters, E E
Blue-collar aristocrats.

Includes bibliographical references and index.
1. Labor and laboring classes—United States.
2. United States—Social conditions—1945— I. Title.
HD8072.L37   301.44'42'0973   74-27309
ISBN 0-299-06550-2

*This book is dedicated to the memory
of the man who owned and operated
The Oasis for a quarter of a century.*

"He was one hell of a swell guy."
*Statement by a regular patron
of the tavern*

Contents

Preface

This is a book about blue-collar men and women who frequent a tavern I choose to call The Oasis. Most of the men work in the various construction trades. I have tried to capture the life-style of these persons so that students and other readers might gain some understanding of them.

We decided at an early stage that the material in this book would have more impact if the actual language of the tavern regulars was retained. Although quotation marks are used it should be remembered that these are the words as I recorded them later—the conversations were not taped. In some places the language of the men has been edited to delete some of the obscenities. The men often modify their language when women are present, and I do not think they would want all of their expressions to appear in print.

Chapter 5, "Battle of the Sexes," was originally published in *The Wisconsin Sociologist* 10 (Spring-Summer, 1973), and chapter 8, "Tavern Social Life," was originally published under the title, "Social Life in a Working-Class Tavern," in *Urban Life and Culture* 2 (April 1973). Both are reprinted here by permission.

Although my wife has always been dubious about "tavern research" she has been relatively tolerant during the period of this study and I wish to thank her for her forbearance.

Finally, I need to thank the men and women of The Oasis for tolerating a middle-classer in their midst during the five years of this study. I hope they like the book and that we can continue to be friends after its publication.

E. E. LeMasters

Madison, Wisconsin
October 1974

BLUE-COLLAR ARISTOCRATS

Introduction

"We decided you were too nice a guy
to be a cop."

*Statement about the author by
a regular patron of The Oasis*

In a society as complex and diverse as that of the United States it is important for behavioral scientists to record and analyze different facets of the social scene. This study attempts to make a contribution to that effort.

The men and women who form the basis of the study were observed in a blue-collar (or so-called "working-class") tavern. The study period was the late 1960s and the beginning of the 1970s— 1967 through 1972. The study group consisted of approximately fifty men and women who were regular patrons of The Oasis,* a family-type tavern. Almost all of the men (over 90 percent) were employed in the construction industry. The trades represented included carpenters, plumbers, bricklayers, roofers, sheet metal workers, plasterers, dry wall specialists, truck drivers, and a few miscellaneous skills. Technically, these men represent the "hard hats" of America—a term they dislike.

The research method used in this study is that of participant-observation. In this approach the researcher attempts to penetrate a social system that he is not a native of, with the hope that he will be able to view the social world of his subjects from the inside rather

*This was not the actual name of the tavern. Names of people and places have been altered.

3

than looking at it from the outside. While there are numerous examples of the use of the participant-observation method in American sociology, an outstanding one is the work of Elliot Liebow as reported in his monograph *Tally's Corner*.[1] Although not black himself, and obviously from the middle class, Liebow gives the reader insight into and feeling for the life of the low income black men he was assigned to study. The book is extremely useful in undergraduate courses for students who have never had any exposure to this segment of American society.

Another excellent example of the participant-observation research method would be the work of Herbert J. Gans as published in his study *The Urban Villagers*.[2] In contrast to Liebow, Gans lived in the section of Boston inhabited by the blue-collar people he was interested in. And in a famous earlier study of blue-collar people in Boston, *Street Corner Society*, William Foote Whyte also moved into the area he was studying.[3]

Some participant-observation studies have been somewhat different in that the social scientist analyzed a social world he had grown up in, using his later training to sort out what seemed to be significant in his earlier experiences. This is the method W. Fred Cottrell employed in his famous monograph *The Railroader*, in which he looked back at his youth in a railroad town in the West.[4] Some of the work of Arnold Green on personality utilized his earlier experiences growing up in a community in New England.[5]

One of the outstanding practitioners of the participant-observation research method has been Erving Goffman. In a series of brilliant studies Goffman has illuminated the complicated and confusing world of the average human being in modern society.[6]

In the present study I was already a resident of Lakeside, the community in which The Oasis tavern is located. As will become apparent in this book, this town was formerly inhabited primarily by blue-collar workers and retired farmers, but since World War II has been the victim (as the natives see it) of a massive invasion by white-collar workers and members of various professions—physicians, engineers, college professors, and the like. Thus, although I was (and am) a resident of the community, I had no ready access to the people who frequent The Oasis. In fact I had three obstacles to overcome before any rapport could be established with the men and women in the tavern: (1) as a newcomer I was part of the invasion resented by the natives (as they see themselves); (2) as a white-collar person I was identified with politicians and other middle-class persons who the blue-collar workers feel have betrayed them in the past; and (3) as a professor I was suspect because at the beginning of this study (about 1965) the nearby campus was torn apart by student-radicals whom the blue-collar persons resented and who they felt should have been restrained by the university administration and the faculty of whom I was a part.

In participant-observation research formal interviews are dispensed with; the data are gathered by observation while the researcher participates in the activities of the group. In this instance I spent as much time as possible at the tavern and attempted to space these visits so that the weekly cycle of events could be experienced. Friday night, for example, is the best time to observe married couples at The Oasis, Saturday morning is unusually rich in "male talk" about hunting and fishing, while holidays such as the Fourth of July often bring entire families to the tavern—parents, children, and even relatives who may be visiting.

Once the group has accepted the observer, two major research problems remain: recording the material and then organizing the data in some fashion that will be useful to behavioral scientists and their students. I attempted to record conversations and events soon after returning home from the tavern—usually within an hour or so. Where possible the exact language of the speaker was used, with some identification of who said what. In recording events (such as a fight) the circumstances surrounding the event were recorded. The recording was by hand, tape recorders were not used.

As the study progressed it became obvious that the material would have to be filed more systematically if it were to make "any sense"—add up to anything. At this point, information was recorded on separate cards or sheets of paper by topic—child rearing, politics, sex, marriage, divorce, and so on. This system eventually resulted in the present organization of the book. Other students of blue-collar life, such as Joseph T. Howell,[7] have used a yearly cycle (winter, spring, summer, fall) in organizing their material, but I feel that such a plan, while interesting to read, makes the data difficult to use. In Howell's excellent study, for example, the reader must make a considerable effort to isolate the material on politics in the book. For this reason the present study is organized by topic. This may have some distortion effect (as Howell thought) but it has the advantage of making the information more accessible.

One of the difficult problems in participant-observation research is that the material is not collected systematically (there are no formal interview schedules or questionnaires), which means that considerable work is required to sort and analyze the data after they are gathered. This means that some theoretical frame of reference has to be decided upon: what are the basic questions of interest to behavioral scientists (or the society) that you are trying to answer? In an English study of affluent blue-collar workers, John H. Goldthorpe and his research team attempted to test the theory of social and cultural homogenization: do skilled manual workers assimilate the life-style of the middle class when they become affluent?[8] The English group concluded that the basic answer was no; within limits the affluent blue-collar workers retain a distinctive life-style of their own.

In this study the basic questions could be stated as follows: (1) To what extent is American society becoming homogenized? Do affluent blue-collar workers retain a distinctive life-style when their income would permit them to emulate the middle class? (2) What functions does the family-type tavern perform in the blue-collar world? In general the study concludes that homogenization in American society may have been overemphasized by some observers. The data to support this conclusion will be found in the various chapters of the book.

In some ways the role of the participant-observer includes two subroles which may be contradictory: in gathering the material the researcher has to be sufficiently gregarious to establish rapport with the people he is writing about, and since he is from a different social world this may require more sociability than some social scientists are capable of. The other subrole, that of analyst, requires theoretical skills that some excellent participant-observers are not adept at. In larger studies these two subroles might be assigned to different persons, but in this study that was not possible.

In attempting to become a member of a group for the purposes of participant-observation research, the researcher has to assume some role in the group to be studied. Goffman, for example, in his study of a mental hospital, points out that in such an institution you are automatically assigned one of three possible roles: you are either a patient in the hospital, a member of the hospital staff, or a visitor.[9] Goffman decided to attach himself to the staff and pretended to be a member of the athletic or recreation department. In his study of low-income families Howell moved into the neighborhood and assumed the roles of neighbor and friend.[10] Liebow, in contrast, identified himself as a social scientist doing research and played that role—but informally he also functioned as a friend when the men in his research group needed help in dealing with agencies in the community.[11]

In this study I initially assumed the role of patron—just another person who liked to drink beer and shoot pool. This finally became difficult because the amount of time I spent in the tavern began to raise questions. Some of the regular customers, I learned later, had decided that I must be an undercover agent for the state liquor commission. When this role definition didn't seem to hold up (one man said, later, "we decided you were too nice a guy to be a cop"), the patrons concluded that I must be an alcoholic who chose to do my drinking at a blue-collar tavern where my professional colleagues would not be likely to see me. This was a reasonable assumption because from time to time, as the study continued, I observed various white-collar professionals with a "drinking problem" who used The Oasis as a refuge from their middle-class associates.

Eventually I adopted the following stance when queried about being in the tavern: that sociologists have to have some knowledge of various aspects of American society to be effective teachers, that I found The Oasis men and women to be helpful in understanding how blue-collar people feel about American society, and, furthermore, that I became bored by constant association with white-collar people and that the tavern contacts were refreshing. All of the above statements were true—the only omission was that I was contemplating a book about The Oasis and its patrons.

After about a year of participating in the life of The Oasis I began to leak the notion that I might be working on a book about the tavern. Some of the patrons took this as a joke and once in a while they would yell: "Hey, Doc, put this in your book." Harry, the owner-proprietor of the tavern, actually knew that a book was contemplated and had agreed to serve as a consultant on the project. Unfortunately, cancer brought his life to an end before the manuscript was ready for discussion but he did answer many questions when the writer was puzzled by some behavior in the tavern.

Eventually, most of the regulars accepted the idea that "Lee is writing a book about us" but most of them did not seem to take the idea very seriously. A few were upset, fearing that something embarrassing about themselves might appear in the book. When two chapters from the book were eventually published in sociology journals most of the patrons seemed to be pleased to see their tavern in the news (even though its name had been changed).*

Some information gathered in a participant-observation study is too intimate for publication—the members of the group would be able to identify the person involved even though other readers would not. Where necessary, material of this nature has been omitted from this published report.

In attempting to enter the world of his research group, the participant-observation worker often needs a sort of "gimmick" which will open the doors for him or her. At The Oasis there are several dedicated pool players and by luck my level of skill at the pool table fitted in with that of the seven or eight better players at the tavern.[12] This resulted in my being asked to shoot as a partner and eventually in my becoming a member of the pool team which represented The Oasis in a metropolitan tavern league. By the end of the study I had played on the team for three seasons.

There are, obviously, many problems involved in using the participant-observation research method.[13] One never knows, for example, how typical or atypical the persons being observed are of their referent group in American society. Were, for example, Whyte's young men typical of their generation in his study *Street Corner Society?* Are most low-income black men like those in Liebow's *Tally's Corner?* As a rule the participant-observation researcher goes into the field *where he can get in,* hoping that the findings will be useful to somebody. Alfred Kinsey faced this same problem when he attempted three-hour interviews with thousands of American men

*Chapter 5 was widely publicized in the mass media.

and women about their private sex lives; when criticized about his sample Kinsey defended his work by saying that the sex researcher has to take the informants he can get.[14] Social and cultural anthropologists have always had this same problem: not all human societies or groups are available for intimate observation by outsiders.[15]

Furthermore, in the participant-observation research method the observer may not be skilled or competent, and it is difficult to determine how reliable the findings are. For example: one of my students once served in Dobu during World War II and claims he did not find the paranoid attitude which Reo G. Fortune, an anthropologist, reported to be typical of these people and their culture.[16]

Another serious problem in this research method is that it is extremely difficult (if not impossible) to replicate these studies.

In view of the many problems in the participant-observation research method, why has it had such a vogue in sociology and anthropology? Why have the works of Goffman, Whyte, Liebow, and others been so widely used in American sociology courses? The answer is that participant-observation research, if well done, gives the reader insight into the lives of the persons being studied and a feeling for these people that cannot be attained through more formal quantitative research. If one reads Cottrell's *Railroader,* for example, it is almost impossible to forget how an occupation can impinge on family life. After an exposure to Goffman's *Asylums* it is unlikely that any intelligent person would fail to remember how a patient must feel in a mental hospital. Liebow's portrait of low income black men in *Tally's Corner* is unforgettable for most readers.[17]

This type of qualitative research does not, of course, diminish the need for quantiative studies—the two research methods supplement each other.

It is hoped that this study will be a contribution toward the ethnography of American society.

1 The Tavern, The Town, and the Professor

"You can always have a good time
at The Oasis."
Statement by a customer at the
tavern

THE TAVERN

The Oasis is not a neighborhood tavern.[1] Its customers arrive in cars, not on foot, some of them from several miles away. They come because the men they work with congregate there. Most of the men are skilled construction workers who stop at the tavern on the way home from work. There is a joke about the "blue-collar cocktail hour"—the joke is that the hour lasts from 5 to 7 P.M. and the beverage is beer, not cocktails.

One reason why the customers know each other so well is that they not only work together but have been coming to this same tavern for ten to fifteen years. In fact, the owner once told me that some of the customers had been coming for the quarter of a century that he had owned and operated the tavern.

In many ways Harry, the owner-proprietor, played the role of the benevolent father, the head of a large family. He knew the wives and children of his regular customers, and also many of their relatives because it was customary to bring family visitors to the tavern "to meet the gang." I once heard him say to a rowdy customer: "This is my home—this is where I spend most of my life. My customers are my friends. Do you understand?"

The owner tried to keep his customers from drinking too much—a battle that he often lost.* I have seen him ask a customer to tend bar

---

*He himself was a moderate drinker. When tending bar he abstained entirely.

11

so he could drive home a regular patron who had had "too much." The regular customers, in turn, not only knew Harry quite well— they also were well acquainted with his wife, his children, and most of his relatives. One of the social functions of such a tavern, as we shall see later, is to protect the individual against the impersonality of the mass society.*

Physically, The Oasis is not very impressive. It occupies the exposed basement of an old two-story building which dates back to the 1880s or 1890s. It is partially hidden by a swanky cocktail lounge and restaurant next door called The Tuxedo. On the other side of the tavern there is a cemetery. As Harry used to say, "The people on the one side don't give us any trouble but once in a while there is a wild party on the other side."

As you enter the tavern there is a horse-shoe shaped bar which seats about thirty customers (depending on how close the owner places the bar stools). The shape of the bar facilitates conversation as most of the customers face each other. To the left, in the corner, is a juke-box. A color television set is perched on a platform in the opposite corner. Used largely for sporting events, it affords a good view from any seat at the bar. A small kitchen opens off the corner by the television set and is used for making sandwiches and heating soup. †

Near the bar, opposite the entrance, is the lady's room, remodeled in recent years and better than many taverns offer (report from some of the female customers). Also to the right from the entrance is a beer cooler from which customers help themselves for take-home cartons or cases. Farther to the right is a three-quarter-size pool table operated by a coin slot—put a quarter in and the balls come out.

Across the room from the pool table is a long shuffleboard, popular with couples because some of the wives are skilled players and enjoy the game (most of them do not shoot pool very often). Beyond the pool table and the shuffleboard, to the right of the entrance, is the men's room—*not* remodeled in recent years and above average for blue-collar taverns. Its location, so far from the

---

*See chapter 8 on tavern social life.
†No complete meals are served, only soup and sandwiches. The soup is made by the owner's wife and is popular with the luncheon customers.

bar, has been the source of many complaints from the male customers. I once heard the following exchange:

"Goddammit, Harry, why in the hell did you put the lady's room so close to the bar and the men's room so far—you know the women don't have to go as often as we do!"

Harry replied: "I did it on purpose—you guys are getting fat and need the exercise."

The customer snorted and hurried toward the men's room.

Scattered around, between the bar, the pool table, and the shuffleboard, are small tables used for eating, drinking, and playing cards. In a far corner, near the men's room, is a coin telephone—placed there to assure privacy. Here and there, space can be found for dancing, although it is not easy when the bar is crowded. This, however, is no insurmountable obstacle to couples who really want to dance.

Outside is a parking lot which holds about twenty cars (this depends somewhat on the amount of alcohol consumed that day by the customers; one St. Patrick's Day only two cars got in—and they met in the middle of the lot).

The Oasis is conveniently located for transient trade (two main streets are adjacent) but relies on its regular clientele for the bulk of its business.

THE TOWN: A RELUCTANT SUBURB

Lakeside is a former rural village in the process of becoming a suburb.[2] When originally settled in the 1820s the town's main function was to serve as a shopping center for the farmers in the surrounding countryside—Metropolis was ten miles away, too far for frequent trips by horse and buggy. In the late nineteenth century prosperous upper-middle-class families living in Metropolis began to build summer homes on the lake shore near the village, commuting to the city via the daily train service. By 1900 the population of the town was about 1200. In the 1920s, with the development of the moderate-priced automobile, blue-collar workers from Metropolis began to buy homes in Lakeside, commuting to the city via the new paved highway.

Over the years a few small industrial plants located in the village, largely because wages and taxes were lower than in the central city. At this stage of its growth the economic base of the community rested on three supports: retail sales to the area's farmers, local industry, and commuters who worked in Metropolis.*

The community followed this same growth pattern until the end of World War II. At this time prosperous middle-class families from the metropolitan center began to infiltrate the community, building single-family homes in the $25,000-$40,000 category. Metropolis was now only fifteen minutes by car, the lake was convenient, and a few wooded areas provided ideal building sites.

At this time a political struggle developed for control of the community: on one side were aligned the original blue-collar residents and numerous elderly persons who had retired in the village, and on the other side were the new white-collar invaders. This struggle centered on control of the school system but had many other ramifications.†

In the 1960s, when this study began, the community was shocked by the construction of several hundred apartment units designed primarily for white-collar employees who worked in Metropolis. While the apartment buildings are physically attractive, their presence has added a more or less transient population that the village never had before. Furthermore, almost all of the apartment dwellers are white-collar, which means that the traditional blue-collar control of the village is more threatened than ever.

By 1960 the population of the town was approximately 6000 and by 1970 was about 8000.††

Sociologically, it would be difficult to find a more interesting community than Lakeside. All of the problems facing America are facing Lakeside—pollution of their beautiful lake, white-collar invasion of their blue-collar town, drugs in the local high school, rising taxes, urban sprawl, the war in Indochina, inflation, the revolt of youth, the desire of women for a better deal, and so on. The tavern

---

*In the 1940s the population of Metropolis was approximately 50,000. As of 1970 this had increased to about 150,000.

†See chapter 10 for an analysis of this struggle.

††In the 1960s the legal definition of the community was changed from "village" to "city."

is a good vantage point from which to study these problems—as the subsequent chapters should demonstrate.

There are numerous taverns in Lakeside in addition to several cocktail lounge-supper club establishments. The taverns are segregated primarily by the age and occupation of their customers—at least two of the taverns cater essentially to young single men and women, most of whom are either students from the nearby state university campus or are white-collar workers from the host of state offices in Metropolis, which is also the state capital.

The other taverns are patronized primarily by middle-aged blue-collar workers and their wives. One of these seems to be dominated by divorced men and their girl friends, while another appears to cater largely to men of somewhat less skill and income than those who do their drinking at the Oasis. I have visited all of the taverns in Lakeside (some of them several times) but have studied only The Oasis intensively.

I was attracted to The Oasis for several reasons: (1) the same person had owned and operated this tavern for over twenty years; (2) not only men but entire families were to be encountered at the tavern at different times; (3) the same people were to be found at the tavern week after week—there was very little transient trade; and (4) the clientele appeared to be highly homogenous in terms of social class and occupation: most of the men were skilled construction workers or public employees at the blue-collar level. It seemed to me than (and now) that this was a group of men and women who would provide a worthwhile view of the stable skilled blue-collar world in American society.

Taverns pass through what might be described as a "life cycle"—at one point in time they are well managed, prosperous, and enjoyable. At another time the same tavern will be in a state of transition—new owner, new customers, new atmosphere. In 1965, when I first discovered The Oasis, this tavern was probably at one of the peaks of its life cycle; the business was prosperous; the owner-operator and his major bartender knew almost all of the customers personally; the patrons were, for the most part, respectable members of the community; most of the regulars knew each other; and one could almost always count on having a "good time" at The Oasis. Samuel Johnson, the legendary English wit, is reported by Boswell to have once paid this tribute to taverns: "There is no private house in which people can enjoy themselves so well, as at a capitol tavern."[3] This seemed to be true of The Oasis in the 1960s.

Later on, the owner-operator developed what turned out to be terminal cancer, the tavern was sold, and many changes took place. The Oasis remained primarily a blue-collar tavern but some of the married couples drifted to other taverns and were seen no more at The Oasis. If some of the material in this study may seem a bit rosy, it might be remembered that The Oasis was a happy place during the early years of this study—as happy a place as one expects to find in the modern world.

THE PROFESSOR

The original genesis of this study was in World War II when I was stationed in an English community for three years while attached to the United States Naval Air Corps. During this period I became fascinated with the English pub (public house) and the functions it performed in English society. It soon became apparent that the pubs in England were highly stratified in terms of the people they served. In this particular urban area, for example, one pub I frequented was patronized almost exclusively by male school teachers (called schoolmasters by the English). Blue-collar workers or upper-middle-lcass persons (such as physicians or attorneys) were rarely encountered in this pub, and most of the patrons were to be seen there night after night.

I eventually became a regular patron of a pub called The Dove, which catered almost exclusively to blue-collar workers who were members of the Labour Party. White-collar workers from the community were seldom seen in The Dove, and the vehement political discussions almost always centered about issues related to the problems of the English working class. It was here that the writer first learned that Winston Churchill and his government would be "turned out" (defeated) once the war was over. This eventually came to pass.

After World War II my brother owned and operated a working-class tavern in a small Ohio rural community. On vacations I would spend hours in this tavern listening to the patrons and discussing them with my brother. On Saturday nights almost the entire village population assembled in the tavern—at that time the bar provided the only television set in town. My brother finally had to set a rule that children under twelve had to be taken home at 11 P.M.

It became apparent that the tavern in this small community was the center of social life and the the proprietor had an amazing amount of knowledge about the residents of the town—he could predict election results, for example, with great accuracy. He also knew what marriages were unstable, what spouse was unfaithful, what teen-age girl was pregnant, and that the new "reform" governor was as corrupt as the previous governor (he knew this because the county political "pay off" man continued to call every month for the fifty-dollar contribution required if the tavern had a slot machine or sold tickets on punch boards, and this after the new governor had been elected on a platform to "end gambling in Ohio").

My father began his adult life as a coal miner, digging coal several hundred feet under ground, working in water all day, for two dollars a day. This was in the soft coal region of eastern Ohio and before the organization of the coal miner's union under John L. Lewis. To the day of his death my father talked about the working conditions of the coal miners when he was down in the mines.

Most of my relatives in Ohio were either blue-collar workers or poor farmers—there were scarcely any prosperous farmers in that part of Ohio during the 1920s or the 1930s. The soil itself was not suitable for farming, and economic conditions were disastrous for farmers.

During a strike in the coal mines my father obtained employment in a grocery store and through a series of fortunate events became a salesman for a wholesale grocery firm. This moved our family into the lower middle class of that community.

The neighborhood in which we eventually located was mixed from a social class point of view. A neighbor across the street was the most prominent criminal lawyer in the region and owned his own string of harness racing horses. Two doors east, also across the street, lived a family that was in the lumber business and eventually became millionaires during World War II. But also in the immediate neighborhood lived two men that the writer chooses to call blue-collar aristocrats—men who were at the top of the so-called working class and who walked down the street with pride and dignity.

One of these men, who lived in the house to the right of us, was a railroad engineer. Train engineers, at that time, were highly paid by local standards (this was a town of 12,000). When the engineer walked to work he was immaculately dressed in his blue overalls, blue shirt, and blue railroader's cap, with his high top black shoes freshly polished.* Under his arm was an ample lunch bucket. It was something just to watch this man walk down the street. This was during the 1920s, when most blue-collar workers were unorganized and poorly paid.

Three doors to our left lived another blue-collar aristocrat—a "roller" in one of the local steel mills. This man, of Irish descent, was the key man in the steel-making process: he decided when the steel was ready for its final finishing. Today this would be done by computer, but then men with experience and skill were the crucial actors in the steel-making process. This roller, by the way, drove the same large Buick (the most expensive model available) as the criminal lawyer across the street.

This background material is inserted to help the reader understand that I have always overlapped two social worlds—that of the blue-collar worker and that of the white-collar worker. I have been a "marginal" person in the sociological sense. The men at The Oasis reminded me of the blue-collar aristocrats I had known as a youth— they were (and are) proud and independent. This was one of the reasons why I decided to write a book about them.

---

*In the 1970s, one of my sons, a university student, adopted a style of dress modeled after that of the railroad engineer, including the cap.

The World of Work

"It's a damn good thing we have the union."
Statement by a carpenter at
The Oasis

INTRODUCTION

Historically, in Western society the center of a man's life was his job. His self-image, and his status in the community, were reflections of how he earned a living. An unemployed man—unless he was wealthy—literally had no position in the society.[1] Even today, when two men meet for the first time, an early question will be: "what do you do?" This is an attempt to place each other in the social structure.

In recent decades in American society (and probably in other urban-industrial societies) it has been hypothesized that work is becoming less central in the lives of men.[2] This idea rests upon two types of evidence: (1) that mechanization of manufacturing, especially in the mass industries such as steel and automobiles, has reduced the average worker to the level of a machine, with monotonous, repetitive operations that produce boredom and a demand for early retirement;[3] and (2) that man (in highly developed societies) can now produce all the *things* he needs in a few hours a day and that he has to look outside his job for the real significance of his life.[4]

In a definitive study of the life of Warren G. Harding, Russell points out that in the early 1920s, when Harding attempted to persuade the American steel industry to adopt the eight-hour day,

19

the reply was that the twelve-hour day and the six-day week were essential for industrial efficiency.[5] Obviously, if a man is on the job seventy-two hours a week his work has to be the center of his life. Today the forty-hour, five-day week has become standard in the United States, and in recent years a few unions have even achieved the thirty-hour week.[6]

It is my belief that the world of work has retained its basic significance for the blue-collar aristocrats in this study. To some extent the rest of this chapter will be an examination of this hypothesis.

JOB SATISFACTION*

In a book that has had a tremendous audience in America, Charles A. Reich makes this statement: "The majority of adults in this country *hate their work.*"[7] This may or may not be true of the average American, but it certainly is not true of the skilled blue-collar workers in this study. In the period of observation being reported on, I never heard a single man say that he hated his work—or even disliked it. Complaints were heard about particular foremen, or the weather on outside construction jobs, but as a group the men seemed to enjoy their work. They joked about incidents on the job, they drank beer after work with members of the crew—and they earned good wages.

Here is a typical conversation. I asked a man at the bar what job he was working on.

"I'm working nights on that new power plant up at Portage."

"What do you do on the job?"

"I'm driving one of the big 'cats'—moving dirt. We have 600,000 cubic yards of earth to move. Man, there are so damn many machines moving dirt up there they should have a traffic cop."

"Do you like the work?"

"Yeah—it's all right once you get used to it. Pays well—we're getting overtime all summer."

This man's work is not monotonous: he has to be alert at all times;

---

*The reader needs to remember that the men in this study had regular employment when these observations were made.

he is responsible for an expensive piece of equipment;* he has no close supervision on the job; he is not about to be replaced by a computer; he belongs to a strong trade union; and with his overtime he earns almost twice as much as a public school teacher.

What are the sources of job satisfaction for these men? They appear to be the following:

The Male Peer Group

The men who frequent The Oasis seem to derive great satisfaction from their daily interaction with other males—both on and off the job. Their talk reflects this.

"Did you see Charlie when he showed up for work Monday? That poor bastard had such a hangover he should have been hospitalized! By noon he had hit his thumb five times with the hammer. He was a mess."

Some of the men ride to work together in car pools; they work in small crews; they eat lunch together; and after work they often have a few beers together. As a result the interpersonal relations are quite significant. They may not always like their crew buddies but the interaction is rich.

The talk reflects the weather on the job, mistakes made on the building site, arguments with the foreman, accidents, practical jokes, and so on.

"Were you on the campus today, Doc?" a concrete worker asked me. "We really had traffic tied up for blocks."

"What happened?"

"We were pumping concrete up to the top floor of that new library by the lake and the goddamn pump went out on us. By the time we got the sonofabitch going again the cement trucks were lined up for half a mile waiting to unload. I'll bet it cost the company $5,000 in overtime before we got out of there tonight."

"Practical jokes" are common in the world of the construction worker. Cars will be tampered with so a worker can't get his started at the end of the day; lunch buckets will be hidden; coffee in a thermos bottle will be replaced with some other liquid; tools will be

*The big earth movers can cost $35,000 and more.

concealed, etc. As a rule this is all in good fun but occasionally fights result from such "horse play." All in all, the male peer life of the skilled blue-collar worker appears to be very rich and meaningful.

The Nature of the Job

The blue-collar aristocrats at The Oasis emphasize several features of their work when they attempt to explain the source of their job satisfaction. The pay, of course, is good. For former farm boys who came out of the depression, with only modest educations, the take-home checks are impressive. In addition they have fringe benefits, paid vacations, and bonus pay for overtime or holiday work (including Saturday or Sunday). They mention that the security of their job is made possible by union membership—seniority rights, protection against arbitrary dismissal, etc.

The men appreciate the fact that their work is not monotonous. A carpenter said: "I see that the auto workers in Detroit want early retirement. I don't blame the poor bastards. I would want to retire at thirty-five if I had to stand in one place and put left fenders on all day."

In construction work (also in truck driving) the men work under relatively loose supervision. "The foreman lays out the day's work in the morning," a plumber said, "and unless we run into trouble we might not see him again all day."

A good carpenter, as a matter of fact, would resent close supervision—this would be a reflection on his competence.

The men like the freedom to move around on the job, also the fact that problems of one kind or another develop almost every day—these "jams" make them think and reassure them that they are not stupid machines.*

In nice weather the men enjoy working outdoors. Most of these men love to hunt and fish and they hate being "cooped up" all day in some building.

The men also get satisfaction from seeing the results of their labor. A carpenter said this: "I tell you, Lee, I get a hell of a kick when I

---

*One is reminded here of the satisfaction astronauts report when they have to correct the work of automatic devices during space flight.

drive around town and see a building I helped to put up. You know that Edgewater Hotel down by the lake? I worked on that sonofabitch fifteen years ago and she's still beautiful. I did the paneling in that dining room that looks out over the water. Sometimes I drive down there just to see the damn thing—do you think I'm nuts or something?"

The Wild Irishman, an excellent pool player, operates the type of crane used in high rise construction. In the 1960s he worked on most of the tall, dramatic university buildings that look out over the lake and now dominate the campus landscape. I once asked the Irishman what it was like to sit at the top of this huge crane and survey the world beneath him.

"Lee," he said, "I wouldn't trade that job for anything in the world. The other day, when I wasn't busy, I took a look around and I could see three different lakes—hell, it was so damn clear I could see the spot near Verona where I shot a pheasant last year."

After another shot of bourbon the Irishman added: "There's only one drawback to being a high rise crane operator."

"What's that?"

"You don't get a good view of the miniskirts on the campus."

In this job the crane operator sits alone in the cab—he has no boss looking over his shoulder. He can communicate with men on the ground via walkie-talkie radio but most communication is by means of hand signals. The job carries great responsibility—at any given moment the crane operator may be lifting a ton of steel or precast masonry over the heads of pedestrians and his fellow workers. An error could easily result in death and/or expensive damage to material. The crane itself will represent an investment of perhaps $100,000.

One of the buildings the Irishman worked on was a beautiful one near my office. I once asked him if it made any difference to him whether a building he worked on was beautiful or not. He decided to have another shot of Early Times before answering. He also paused long enough to buy a fresh can of Copenhagen snuff.

"Doc," he said, "it's just like going out with a woman. I can enjoy her whether she's pretty or not—but by God it does help if she's easy to look at.

"Now you take that building near your office—isn't she a beautiful sonofabitch? When we put that top floor on and you could begin to see her final shape I felt good all over. It's nice to think that when I'm dead and gone that sonofabitch will still be there looking out over the lake and as pretty as ever."

Integrity

Last, but not least, these blue-collar aristocrats actually feel that they are earning an "honest living"—that working with your hands is more honorable than "shuffling papers" or earning a living "with your mouth." They recognize the integrity of a good architect or that of a construction engineer, but they still feel that a great many white-collar workers make no substantial contribution to the welfare of our society.

In some ways this type of thinking reflects the farm background of these men—on the farm you milked the cows, cleaned the barn, plowed the field, harvested the crops.[8] As in construction work there was always physical evidence of what you had done or hadn't done—nobody could pretend they had plowed the field when in fact they had not. Similarly, a bricklayer can't pretend he set six hundred bricks when in fact he did not.

This attitude on the part of these men poses some very real problems in the modern era. As American society becomes increasingly white-collar these men become more and more cynical—they don't trust their labor leaders (who are white-collar) nor do they trust their political leaders (who are also white-collar). Furthermore, it is not enough that a man formerly worked with his hands—"now the sonofabitch works with his mouth."

On another level, these men do *physical* labor—they lift and carry and strain and sweat. While modern construction work does employ machines, laying brick, throwing mud (plaster), or finishing concrete have not changed drastically in the lifetime of these men. Thus, at the end of a day they *know* they have done a day's work. Their clothes and their bodies testify to the fact. These men do not understand or appreciate the type of pressure and sweat that accompany many white-collar jobs. They figure that "the sonofabitch has a soft job" and diminish their respect accordingly.

They make exceptions, of course. One carpenter, for example, said this about being president of the United States: "That job is a sonofabitch. I feel sorry for the poor bastard." But this man does not concede the same consideration to the president of the state university system or the governor of the state.

Essentially, the major problem in the attitude of these men toward work is a form of smugness. In effect they say to me (and to the vast majority of white-collar workers): "I do an honest day's work and you don't." This is not very helpful in a society that is becoming increasingly white-collar.

UNEMPLOYMENT, INJURY, AND SICKNESS

The real significance of work for these men can be seen (and even felt) when they are unemployed because of illness, injury, or lack of work. A plasterer, for example, developed tuberculosis and had to be hospitalized for several months. When he was able to resume his visits to the tavern he said this: "Jesus Christ! I almost went nuts out at that sanatorium. All my goddamn life I've been throwing mud, and to sit on my ass for three months was almost too much for me." He added that the recreational therapy program at the sanatorium had been his salvation—he made lamps and lamp shades that were sold at the tavern during his hospitalization.

A carpenter broke a foot when a scaffold collapsed and was unable to work for several months. Most of this time he spent at the tavern and seemed to be miserable.

"The problem," he said, "is that I feel so goddamn good and yet I can't go to work. With these damn crutches I can't do hardly anything."

"You could catch up on your sex life," a customer at the bar suggested.

"I've already done that. The old lady said yesterday she wished I'd go back to work so she could get some rest."

"Sure wish I could break my foot and get some extra screwing," another man at the bar said.

"You'd be damn sorry if you did," the carpenter replied.

An unemployed electrician made this statement: "Sonofabitch if I'm not tired of loafing. I've painted the damn house inside and out, I've polished the car until the paint is almost off—I'm going nuts waiting to go back to work." This man finally had to sell his new house and move his family to Florida to find work at his trade.

One of the reasons why being unable to work disturbs these men is the fact that the lay-off was not their choice—they are not in control of the situation. When deer season opens—or pheasant season—these men love to take a week or two off without pay and think nothing of it. But when circumstances beyond their control force a lay-off they become upset.

There are other reasons why a forced interruption of work disturbs these men:

1. The tend to drink more when they don't work. Many of these men have what might be called "a drinking problem," which they control, at least in part, by not drinking on the job eight hours a day, five days a week. Unemployment upsets the delicate balance of their drinking program—partly because they spend more time at the tavern when they are not working.

2. The marital relationships of some of these men seem to become "tense" when the husband is unemployed. The wives are not accustomed to having their husbands home very much during the daytime, with the result that normal routines are disrupted. The husband, being upset by his inability to work, is not, of course, at his best in his marital role during this period.

3. Financial problems develop when a man is unable to work for any length of time. Unemployment compensation and disability pay help but the income is not what it is when full employment is enjoyed.

The basic point is that one of the best indicators of the importance of the job to these men is their discomfort when they can't work.

SOCIAL CLASS MOBILITY

In reading about American society one sometimes gets the impression that all Americans are assumed to be "strivers"—struggling to get ahead, to rise in the social class structure.[9] This does not appear to be true of the blue-collar elite in this study. Their attitude toward social class mobility will be examined in this section.

Upward Mobility

Most of the men at The Oasis seem to be relatively content with their lot in this world. Given their limited educational background, most of them feel that their job is about as good as they could expect. A few of the men have attempted to move up in the economic system, usually by starting their own business, and one or two have succeeded,* but most of them gave up the attempt for one reason or another.[10]

"Hell," said the Wild Irishman, "I've owned my own business two or three times. I was in the trucking business for two or three years and I owned a tavern for awhile—in fact that's where I learned to shoot pool better than you guys" (wink).

"Why did you give up your own business?"

"It was too damn much trouble. The trucking business interfered with my drinking and the tavern kept me from hunting—I couldn't find anybody honest to run the place while I went away on hunting trips."

This man's life-style maximizes independence and freedom, values not easily achieved operating a small business. He is now a well-paid crane operator—"a job that suits me fine," he says.

Another patron of The Oasis, a roofer, admits that he failed when he attempted to become a roofing contractor. "I got involved with one of these real estate developers and got a contract to roof twenty-seven houses for him. When half of the houses were done I went to collect some money and the guy stalled me off—said he would have the money in two or three weeks. I wasn't really worried because I knew the sonofabitch had a lot of money."

"What happened?"

"Well, the bastard took the bankrupt law and I lost almost every cent. It seemed that this new development was a separate corporation and we couldn't touch the rest of his money. I finally got a lawyer and he explained the bankruptcy law to me."

"Did you ever get your money?"

"About five cents on the dollar. The bastard cleaned me out."

*You do not usually see the upwardly mobile at The Oasis because they now patronize middle-class bars.

This man then went back to work as a roofer. He admits that he didn't have the knowledge to compete with experienced business operators.

One man at The Oasis has become a successful entrepreneur and still frequents the tavern.

"I started out with one truck," he says, "hauling to California and back—about two weeks for a round trip."

"What did you haul?"

"Everything. You name it and I hauled it. Everything from cheese to fertilizer."

This man eventually acquired a fleet of trucks and has also developed some real estate projects.

"How do you like owning your own business?"

"Terrific—it gives you a chance to work seven days a week and fifteen hours a day—I wouldn't miss it for the world."

He looked around the bar. "See how sad all these guys look? That's because they only get to work forty hours a week. Bartender! Give all these guys a drink—they don't look happy."

An interesting fact about this man is that his life-style remained substantially the same after he became affluent; he and his wife still use The Oasis as the center of their social life, most of their friends are blue-collar workers, and they still live in the same neighborhood.

The owner of the tavern is a good illustration of social class mobility. During World War II Harry managed a shoe department in a large department store. At the end of the war he purchased The Oasis and has now operated it successfully for twenty-five years. The customers are convinced that Harry is "well fixed" financially.

Regardless of his financial status, Harry's values are those of the farm he grew up on. He believes in hard work, honesty, and frugality. "Hard work never hurt anybody," Harry says. "One of the problems today is that a lot of people want a good living but they don't want to work for it."

Harry feels that his boyhood on a farm during the depression was a great advantage for him.

"Lee," he once said to me, "I never expected much out of life—things looked pretty bleak on the farm in 1933. Then, when I got a good job during the war and made a little money I felt like a king. After that I found a nice girl to marry and we had two fine daughters and I could hardly believe that this could happen to old Harry."

Harry points out that in the early years of The Oasis he and his family had to live upstairs over the tavern because he didn't have enough money to buy a house. "All of my money was in the business." He often worked seven days a week behind the bar and fifteen hours a day until his finances allowed him to hire more help. Now he usually doesn't work evenings, week-ends, or holidays. He owns a nice home in a pleasant section of Lakeside.

"Sometimes I feel sorry for the young guys who come in here," Harry says. "Some of them think they have the world by the tail and they're due for a rude awakening some day. I learned that lesson early—on the farm during the depression."

One has the impression that most of the men at The Oasis would not be willing to endure the tension and responsibility described by Harry and the truck owner earlier in their climb up the economic ladder. Leisure and the freedom to enjoy life hold high priority in the life-style of the tavern regulars, and most of them would be reluctant to sacrifice these values just to earn more money.

The above attitude can be seen in the view these men take of overtime—even when it pays time and a half or double time.

"Goddammit!," one plumber said, "the boss wants me to work again this Saturday—that's three Saturdays in a row. I told him that next Saturday I'm going fishing whether he wants me to work or not."

You sometimes get the impression that some of the wives at the tavern wish their husbands were more ambitious. One wife remarked: "My husband wouldn't give up his hunting and fishing if they offered to make him governor—he'd say, 'to hell with it.' "

Some of these men have seen buddies crack up after being promoted to a supervisory position.* "He is a helluva good man but I don't think he'll live over five more years. He developed ulcers the first year they promoted him and the doctors had to take out part of his stomach. Then he got to drinking too much and now he's taking pills by the

---

*A job superintendent has responsibility for the daily operations at the construction site. This is usually a worker who has been promoted from the ranks—not an engineer or an architect.

handful. His doctor told him to quit the job but he's too damn stubborn—like the other Krauts in here" (this last with a wink).

As a group the men seem well satisfied with their position in American society. They feel that they earn an honest living and at the end of the day they can see what they have accomplished. One man said: "When I hang a door or install a kitchen cabinet I like to think that that sonofabitch will still be there long after I'm gone."

Downward Mobility

You seldom see a man at The Oasis who has lost his place in the blue-collar aristocrat world—such men gravitate to taverns which cater to a lower status group. In talking with a few of these men who strayed into the tavern from time to time we had the impression that three factors seemed to have contributed to their downward mobility: (1) marital problems and/or divorce; (2) alcoholism or a "drinking problem"; and (3) illness or injury resulting from some type of accident.

"I used to come in here all the time," one man said. "I was a cement finisher then. But I got arthritis and had to go on disability. I get a check every month but, hell, it ain't what I used to make on concrete."

"You ever been to Joe's tavern on the other side of town?" he asked. "It's not a bad place."

One afternoon I stopped in at Joe's for a beer. As expected, most of the men at the bar appeared to be either disabled or retired. The former concrete finisher would feel comfortable there. The Oasis is not very pleasant for such a person—all around him are the healthy guys making the money he used to make and having the fun he used to have.

In a society in which everybody is supposed to be "on the make," downward mobility must be an extremely painful experience. This certainly appears to be true at The Oasis.

Conclusion

In summary, one would have to agree with Bennett M. Berger and John H. Goldthorpe that the blue-collar elite do not expect to rise in the class structure as individuals; they pin their hopes on collective bargaining to improve their lot as a member of the working class.[11]

SOCIAL CLASS MARGINALITY

In *The Sociology of Subcultures* David O. Arnold concludes that many Americans reflect more than one social class position: they overlap two or more social class life-styles.[12] In this chapter references were made earlier to a man who had become affluent in the trucking business but who still spends most of his time with blue-collar friends.

Another marginal person at The Oasis has owned several businesses in his lifetime but is now employed as a butcher. "During World War II I made a lot of money selling used cars to defense workers. Those guys were making more dough than they knew what to do with and it was easy to take it away from them." He paused to order another shot of whiskey.

"Then I retired, moved to Florida, and those guys down there took my money away from me. Now I'm back cutting meat—where I started twenty years ago."

At one time this man owned championship show horses. "I had a horse named Princess that won every damn ribbon in this part of the country—I kid you not. She was a beautiful horse and she died."

After another drink he added: "I loved that horse. She meant more to me than most people do."

This man grew up in the blue-collar world, moved into the white-collar world, and is now back in the blue-collar ranks.

There are other patrons of The Oasis who overlap two or more social class worlds. Some of these are moving up in the social class system, others are moving down, and some tend to fluctuate from one social class position to another. In general my data on this point tend to support the finding by Arnold cited earlier.

ECONOMIC CONSUMPTION PATTERNS

In their studies of the affluent blue-collar worker in England after World War II the Goldthorpe research group concluded that these men do not buy consumer items just to impress their neighbors; they spend their money on better housing and things such as refrigerators which actually improve the convenience and/or quality of their daily life.[13] It is my belief that this is also true of the skilled blue-collar workers examined in this study.

A good illustration of this is the conspicuous absence of new automobiles in the tavern parking lot. Most of these men are good mechanics—or their friends are—and they tend to keep their cars for several years. As a rule they do not buy new cars: they shop around for a good used one. These patterns would not exist if the automobile functioned as a status symbol for these men.

One Saturday morning The Wild Irishman drove into the parking lot with what appeared to be an expensive new Ford. When he sat down at the bar I asked him when he had bought the new car.

"Hell, that's not new, Doc," he said. "A friend of mine traded it in and I got it for $1500 less than what it cost last year. Only has 19,000 miles on it."

I asked if he ever bought new cars.

"No, I gave that up a long time ago. The depreciation the first year is too high—I'd rather let the other guy take that."

He went on to explain that he always buys his used cars from the same dealer in the small nearby community that he grew up in— usually a car driven by somebody he knows.

A year later I asked him how the car had turned out. "Fine," he said. "Runs like a clock."

The point is that automobiles do not constitute a status symbol with these men. In contrast, a beautiful new pick-up truck is something to brag about.

"You see that new red pick-up out there?" a plasterer said. "That sonofabitch rides like a rocking chair. I damn near broke my ass with that bastard I had before." Several men at the bar went out to take a look at the new truck.

The men often talk about used cars they have their eyes on. "There's a guy on the job driving a 1960 Pontiac that looks terrific. I looked it over the other day and it only has 62,000 miles on it—he's the original owner. This guy needs a heavier car to haul a trailer he's planning to buy. I sure hope to get that sonofabitch when he's ready to sell it."

A status object (not merely a symbol) with these men would be a beautiful deer rifle—not necessarily new. This sort of possession a man would bring to the tavern for his friends to admire.

A pheasant shooting expedition to the Dakotas in the fall would reflect glory on a man at The Oasis. "I never saw so many goddamn birds in my life," one man reported upon returning from such a trip. "We got the limit every day, hunting only about an hour each time." "By God that's the kind of hunting I like," a man at the bar said. "Leaves plenty of time for drinking."

A good fishing boat and motor, a hunting cabin "up north"—these are things that a man cherishes at The Oasis.

It is my belief that the purchasing power of the construction workers in this study has increased faster than their desire for consumer items: the "things" they want in this world are now readily available to them. Many of thier wives also work (about 50 to 60 percent in this group at any given time), and in addition these men have not become addicted to some of the middle-class norms which might pose financial problems for them—for example, they don't feel that every child should go to college.*

The above statements do not apply to the divorced men who frequent The Oasis, nor would these generalizations apply to men who have been unable to work or have experienced some costly tragedy in their family. I do think that the so-called "average" worker in this group lives within his income and feels comfortable with his standard of living.

ATTITUDES TOWARD TRADE UNIONS

Over 90 percent of the blue-collar workers who frequent The Oasis are members of trade unions.[14] The men tend to be realistic about the need for labor unions: they realize that they would be at the mercy of their employers if they were not organized. One bricklayer said: "We would get a good screwing from those bastards if we didn't have a union." He was, of course, referring to the employers.

There is no idealism or social reform content in the talk of these men about their unions: they see them as a means of improving wages, fringe benefits, and working conditions. They do not think of the union as an instrument for social change or social reform. This same view of the union was found in the English studies of affluent blue-collar workers by the Goldthorpe research group.[15]

One of the most negative aspects of trade unionism in the con-

*See chapter 7 for further discussion of child rearing and attitudes toward children.

struction industry as observed at The Oasis is the attitude of the men toward their union officers and leaders. The attitude is one of complete cynicism. "The bastards are in it for what they can get out of it," a truck driver said. "And that's the same reason why I'm in the union."

One factor in the attitude of these men toward union officials is that the union officers have become white-collar workers—people who earn their living "shuffling papers" or "with their mouth." This places the union leaders in the same category as politicians in the eyes of these blue-collar workers.

Historically, of course, craft unions in the United States, unlike industrial unions such as the Automobile Workers, have been conservative (if not reactionary) for a long time. If the men at The Oasis are at all representative it is difficult to see how any social reform could emanate from craft unions.

TRENDS IN THE CONSTRUCTION INDUSTRY

Some of the older workers at The Oasis can see that the construction industry is not what it once was—the emphasis today is on production and volume, not craftmanship. A skilled carpenter put it this way:

"You take those apartments we're working on now. There's 120 units, almost exactly alike. The kitchen cabinets come completely finished. All we do is hang 'em on the wall. The goddamn foreman doesn't care how well we do the job—he wants volume. He has orders to complete so many units this week and by God that's what he does, whether the work is done right or not."

He paused to order another beer. "The younger men don't mind it—that's the way they were trained. But my old man taught me how to be a carpenter and by God when you cut a piece of wood for the old man it either fit or else. He was particular as hell."

After a few moments of reflection he added: "I don't enjoy the work any more."

SUMMARY AND CONCLUSIONS

For the blue-collar aristocrats in this study the job is still the center of their world. Unlike factory assembly line workers, most of the men at The Oasis still seem to enjoy their work.

In a society that is becoming increasingly white-collar these blue-collar workers distrust the middle-class white collarites and are antagonistic toward them. This attitude influences the feeling of these men toward their union leaders and also toward public officials (this point will be developed in chapter 10).

As America becomes more and more computerized and mechanized and as jobs become more routine, these men emerge as a sort of remnant of a world that is fast disappearing. Some of the men realize this but others would prefer not to think about it.

3 Marriage: Until Death Do Us Part

"My husband is a real nice bastard."
Statement by a happily married woman at The Oasis

INTRODUCTION

In this chapter the focus will be on the marriages at The Oasis which have endured—some of them for fifty years. How do the couples view each other after two or three decades of marriage? Why have these particular marriages survived when so many of the customers at the tavern have been divorced at one time or another? Mirra Komarovsky and others have commented on the stress which seems to characterize blue-collar marriage in our society.[1] To what extent is this marital strain apparent at The Oasis?

In the chapter to follow the divorced persons at the tavern will be analyzed. A separate chapter will be devoted to the way in which the two sexes view each other.

THE MEN VIEW MARRIAGE

Some of the men at The Oasis are quite caustic in their views on marriage, but this is not necessarily a complaint about their marital partners: it is a commentary on either (a) the marriage system, or (b) the nature of the opposite sex.

Here is how one man put it:

"What the Hell Are You Going to Do?"

One day at The Oasis I was wearing a necktie. One of the regular customers spotted the necktie immediately and said: "Damn it, Doc, I wore one of them things once—when I got married—and look what

36

happened to me! By God, the undertaker will have to put the next one on."

It is typical that a necktie symbolizes marriage to this man. He has a very gloomy view of marriage as a way of life.

"They say married people live longer," he said one day, "but I think it just *seems* longer."

I once asked him why he got married when he views marriage with such lack of enthusiasm.

"What the hell you going to do?" he replied. "You just can't go on shacking up with girls all your life—I did plenty of that when I was single."

He paused to order another beer. "A man, sooner or later, likes to have a home of his own, and some kids, and to have that you have to get married. There's no way out of it—they got you hooked."

I said that his wife seemed to be a nice person.

"Oh, hell," he said, "she's not a bad kid, but she's a goddamn woman and they get under my skin.

"They piss me off. If you go to a party, just when you start having fun the wife will say—'let's go home. The children will be worried.'

"Or if you get aroused and want to jump into bed the wife will say—'be quiet, don't wake up the children.' "

He lit a cigarette and then said: "If a woman gives her husband a piece of tail once a week she thinks she is doing him a helluva favor. I don't see it that way."

He also objects to his mother-in-law. "Hell, she comes about three times a year and stays six or seven weeks. She and my wife jabber away like a couple of monkeys—'Uncle Joe died' and all that crap. I get sick of it."

It seems clear that this man is not really complaining about his wife—he is unhappy with *marriage.* He also prefers men as a species to women; except for sexual purposes, he finds women dull and uninteresting. This is not the sort of man who would consider divorce. He is smart enough to know that he would find another wife just as restraining as this one. He also knows that he does not want to go through life as a bachelor.

"Where Can You Find One Any Better?"

"My wife is a good gal, but I just don't know anybody I'd like to be married to for thirty years."

This man was "celebrating" his thirtieth wedding anniversary when he made this statement. He has enough insight to know that divorce and remarriage would not solve any of his problems.

"I don't see any big bargains for an old duffer like me," he said. "I'm better off with what I've got—at least I *know* what those problems are."

This man is not bitter about the institution of marriage, he is philosophical about it. Things have not turned out in his marriage exactly as he had hoped, but he realizes that life in general has not been exactly what he visualized in his youth.

"I got married young—I was only nineteen. What the hell does a kid of nineteen know about *anything,* let alone marriage? As dumb as I was it could have turned out a lot worse."

This man, in his late forties, has only one major complaint about his marriage: that his wife does not share his enthusiasm for The Oasis. "She comes with me once in a while but as a rule she stays home. She doesn't seem to enjoy the place as much as I do."

This man expects to spend the rest of his life with the woman he married thirty years ago.

"I've seen a lot of divorced guys in here and they don't seem so damn happy. I'm gonna stick with what I've got."

This man is shrewd, cautious, and wary in his approach to life. Whether he is shooting pool, shopping for a car, or looking at marriage, he calculates the odds and acts accordingly. He tends to view divorce as a bigger gamble than marriage: "what the hell, if you get divorced the chances are you'll end up with somebody else's castoff. What's so great about that?"

Another man had this to say about his marriage: "My wife has an even temper—she's always mad. If I stick around the house, she says 'why don't you go up to The Oasis?' Then when I come up here she says 'why don't you stay home once in a while?' She's hard to figure out."

But some of the husbands at the tavern are more positive about their marriage.

"A Pretty Good Kid"

The speaker is a large man—they sometimes call him The Peacemaker at The Oasis. When a fight starts he can sometimes stop it just by asking the battlers, "What's all the trouble here?" The men were talking about marriage. This man spends a considerable amount of time at The Oasis and I wondered how he managed this with his wife.

"Oh, my wife gets peed off at me every once in a while for coming over here, but she always gets over it."

After ordering another glass of beer he continued. "My wife is a pretty good kid. She knew I was wild when she married me but I've tamed down a lot since then."

After a few moments he added: "She could have it a lot worse— this way she can always find me when she wants me because this is the only tavern I ever go to.

"And another thing," he added, "she knows damn well when I'm at The Oasis I'm not chasing some beautiful blonde—have you ever seen any in here?"

I said that while some of the women who patronized The Oasis were attractive that it had never been known as a pick-up spot.

"You can say that again, Doc," he said.

This is a man who enjoys male companionship. He likes to drink beer, shoot pool, play cards, pitch horseshoes, bowl, fish, hunt, and talk—activities that center around The Oasis and his male friends there. He wants the enjoyment that the tavern offers as well as the advantages of marriage. About once a week his wife spends an evening with him at The Oasis, and they are close friends of some of the other couples who patronize the tavern.

The Proprietor Views Marriage

"When you operate a tavern for over twenty years you see a lot of marriages come and go, and unless you're completely stupid you should learn something."

The speaker was the owner and proprietor of The Oasis. His own marriage has survived over three decades and appears to be successful.

One afternoon, when the tavern was almost deserted, I asked Harry what his thoughts were on marriage.

"Well," he said, "I suppose I should be gloomy in view of some of the lousy marriages I have seen in here the past twenty years—but I'm not."

He paused to serve a customer who had just walked in.

"The reason I'm not gloomy about marriage," he continued, "is that I've seen what happens to some of these guys when they leave their wife and kids; most of them start to drink too much, begin chasing women, and the first thing you know they're in trouble. I've seen that happen to quite a few men in the past twenty years.

"Another thing, Lee," he said. "Some of the women these divorced guys bring in here seem worse to me than their former wives. I can't see that most of them improve the situation very much when they trade the old one in on a later model."

He chuckled and said: "You know what old Harry is like—when he trades he plans to trade *up*, not *down*."

After cleaning off part of the bar he continued his observations. "Of course, I recognize that some couples have problems that are too much for them, but I still think that most of them could work things out if they tried hard enough."

"You've been married to one woman for a long time," I said. "How did you make a go of it?"

"Well, I can tell you it wasn't always easy," he said. "We didn't have much money when we first got married and my wife had a lot of illness. We had to struggle along until the doctors found out what the trouble was.

"I think the secret of marriage is give and take"—he smiled—"you have to give a lot and sometimes, by God, you have to take a lot!"

He served a customer. "You know, Lee, I grew up on a farm and we never had much—except a helluva lot of hard work. Then, when I moved into town, the damn depression came along and I couldn't get a good job. So, you see, I never expected much from life, and maybe that's why I appreciate my wife, my kids, and this business."

Later on he laughed and said: "When we first got married I was selling shoes in a women's shoe store—and that's a job that makes a man appreciate a good wife. Did you ever watch women buying shoes?"

I confessed that this was one aspect of modern America that had escaped my attention.

"Well, I'll clue you in," he said. "There is something about buying shoes that brings out the worst in a woman—they will bitch when a shoe fits them perfectly and looks good on them. I have had wealthy women come in that store on Friday, take an hour of my time trying on shoes, take a pair home on approval, wear them to some special party, *and return them on Monday for credit!*

"I know damn well they wore them because you can always tell," he added.

"Anyhow," he said, "after a day selling shoes to bitches like that your wife looks pretty good—even if she isn't Hedy Lamarr."

I remarked that Hedy wasn't looking too good these days, judging by the newspaper pictures.

Harry's eyes lit up—he saw an opening.

"Let me tell you something," he said. "You and I aren't getting any prettier either."

In a very real sense some of the men at The Oasis resent marriage because it impinges on their freedom and independence. At the same time they also realize that marriage to another woman would not solve any of their problems. As they often say, "you can't live with 'em and you can't live without 'em."

THE WOMEN VIEW MARRIAGE

How do the wives at The Oasis view marriage? It should be remembered that all of these women have been married for at least fifteen years—most of them longer than that—and that these women are still married to their first husband. It might also be remembered that the bulk of these marriages took place during or right after World War II, when the divorce rate in the United States was quite high.

"What a Drag"

"When I was a young girl I couldn't wait to get married—I thought it was the most wonderful thing in the world. Now I have my doubts."

The speaker is a woman who has been married for about thirty years. She has two grown children but no grandchildren as yet.

"The men go to work while the wife stays home with the kids—it's a long day with no other adult to talk to. That's what drives mothers to the soap operas—stupid as they are.

"Then the husband stops at some tavern to have a few with his buddies from the job—not having seen them since they left to drive home ten minutes ago. The poor guy is lonely and thirsty and needs to relax before the rigors of another evening before the television set."

She paused to sip her beer.

"Meanwhile," she continued, "the little woman has supper ready and is trying to hold the kids off 'until Daddy gets home so we can all eat together.' After a while she gives up this little dream and eats with the kids while the food is still eatable.

"About seven o'clock Daddy rolls in, feeling no pain, eats a few bites of the over-cooked food, sits down in front of the TV set, and falls asleep."

She ordered another beer. Then she said: "This little drama is repeated several thousand times until they have their twenty-fifth wedding anniversary and then everybody tells them how happy they have been.

"And you know what?" she added. "By now they are both so damn punch drunk neither one of them knows whether their marriage has been a success or not."

After a pause to light a cigarette, she said: "I think it's very funny—but I'm not laughing very hard."

I asked her why women seemed so anxious to marry in view of the gloomy state of marriage in our society.

"I don't really know," she said, "but I think it is their desire for children. My children have meant a great deal to me and that is the part of marriage that women like most, in my opinion."

This woman says that she has urged her children not to rush into marriage, but to take their time.

"If You Ask Me, It's a Hell of a Raw Deal"

One wife who frequents The Oasis with her husband has some rather caustic comments on marriage in our society. This woman has been married for twenty-five years to a man who is one of the best-liked men who frequent the tavern. Her remarks, therefore, should be understood as applying primarily to *the marriage system* rather than to her particular marital partner.

"If you ask me," she said one evening, "it's a hell of a raw deal.

The wife has to raise the kids, take care of the house, jump into bed whenever the husband feels like it—and lots of times she has to hold down a job besides."

She paused to light a cigarette, and we all had another round of beer.

"They say that marriage is a 50-50 proposition," she went on, "—that is a pipe dream if I ever heard one. Seventy-thirty in favor of the man would be more like it."

I asked her why most women seemd to want to be married in view of her version of the American marriage system.

"Because they're so damn stupid!" she exclaimed. "They're afraid somebody will call them an old maid some day and so they grab the first jerk that comes along."[2]

She was asked what she thought about the part that sex plays in marital success or failure.

She paused to think a minute. Then she said: "Sex is the most overrated thing in our society—most women can take it or leave it but the men have to hit the sack a couple times a week or they'll cry.

"You know what," she said, "I'd like to give a lecture to that marriage class of yours—I could tell them a thing or two."

I said she would be welcome to give a lecture some time and wondered what points she would stress.

"By God, I'd tell those girls to take their time getting married and to have their fun then—they sure as hell won't have it later."

"What would you tell the young men in the class?"

"I'd tell them not to think they're God's gift to women. Most men seem to think they're doing the girl a favor when they marry her. As I see it, it's just the other way around."

Somebody asked her to dance and that was the end of the proposed lecture to the marriage course.

Some of the women at The Oasis are more philosophical about marriage; they stress its advantages rather than its disadvantages.

"I don't know what I really expected," one wife said, "but it hasn't been exactly a bed of roses, I can tell you. But at the same time I wouldn't want to be single—all those gals are trying to bag a husband. Even the divorced women who come in here are all anxious to get married—and you'd think they would know better."

She paused to light a cigarette. "My husband is not perfect," she

said, "but he's a lot better than some of the men I know. I would
say he is a real nice bastard." At this point she left the bar to play a
game of shuffleboard.

"It's Like Being a Widow"

Some of the women at The Oasis are married to truck drivers.
Most of these men are members of the powerful Teamsters' Union
and have an excellent pay scale, with numerous fringe benefits, but
for the women whose husbands are in long-haul trucking it is a
lonely life.

One woman put it this way: "It's almost like being a widow. My
husband is home about twenty-four hours a week. Last night he
called from Omaha and said he'd be home Saturday night. Then
Monday morning he'll be off to St. Louis or some place like that.

"If something happens to the kids, or the furnace goes bad, I'm
there all alone. It's no picnic, I can tell you."

'Would you marry another truck driver?"

"Not in my right mind," she said.

Essentially, the wives at The Oasis whose marriages have survived
do not focus their complaints on their particular marital partner;
they complain about what seems to them to be inequities in the
marital system. They agree with Jessie Bernard that marriage in
modern America is a better deal for men than it is for women.[3]

SOURCES OF STRESS IN THESE MARRIAGES

In their research on the affluent blue-collar worker in England
after World War II, the Goldthorpe research group concluded that
the men in their sample had adopted the companionate or "togetherness" type of marriage usually associated with the white-collar
middle class.[4] This is not true of the blue-collar elite men in my
sample. These men definitely prefer segregated sex roles, with the
women assuming primary responsibility for child rearing and home
management. This finding is similar to that of Komarovsky, Herbert
J. Gans, and Patricia Cayo Sexton.[5]

Gans makes the important point that marriages based on segregated sex roles can be quite stable and satisfying if both sexes accept the arrangement—as they did in the Italian section of Boston studied by Gans.[6] In the present study, and also in some others,[7] there are signs of strain in these intact marriages that need to be examined. In my opinion the sources of strain are as follows:

1. The men don't want to be "domesticated"; they want the advantages of marriage without the disadvantages. In particular, they want to retain their freedom and independence and their right to spend time with their male buddies when they feel like it. This latter is a constant source of humor at the tavern when a wife telephones her husband. "If that's for me," some man will shout, "tell her I just left—or that I haven't been here." And somebody will almost inevitably say: "I'll bet that's the old battle-axe calling. I'm supposed to be home fixing the stove" (or something of that order).

Just as these men have never learned to like the city, they have also never learned to like the "bonds of matrimony." This does not mean that they don't like (or even love) their wives—it means that they don't like the *institution* of marriage. As they sometimes put it: "Marriage is a wonderful institution—but who wants to live in an institution?"

2. A second source of stress in these marriages is that the wives are closely bound to children and the home. Even though most of the wives hold outside jobs at one time or another, the fact remains that a "good woman" does not neglect her children and her home—the roles of mother and homemaker have high priority in her life style.

The stress arises from the fact that the men have a different set of priorities. For them the roles of occupation and male peer group member are dominant, which sets up a direct conflict with the priority system of the wives.

3. A third source of stress in these intact marriages is a difference in social class identification between the husbands and their wives. In a study of blue-collar wives employed in white-collar jobs, Ernest Barth and Walter Watson concluded that the life-style of the wives was altered to some extent by their exposure to the white-collar world in their jobs.[8] This appears to be true of the wives at The Oasis. At one time or another almost all of these women have worked outside the home but only one of them, to my knowledge,

has ever held a blue-collar job.* The women are cashiers, book-keepers, clerks, telephone operators, typists, beauty operators—jobs which require the development of interpersonal skills with both sexes. In contrast, their husbands work in an all-male one-sexed world and spend their days handling *things* rather than people.[9]

In addition, the wives are exposed to middle-class norms via television, magazines, radio, and mass advertising. The net result of all this seems to be differential socialization between the women and the men: the men love the traditional world they grew up in whereas the women can see some advantages in the white-collar version of "togetherness" in marriage. These sex differences will be explored further in the chapters on marital failure and child rearing.

STRENGTHS IN THESE MARRIAGES

In view of the stresses discussed above, why (or how) have these marriages survived? The writer would suggest the following reasons:

1. These men, being at the top of the blue-collar world, represent a good "catch" for the average girl. A plumber or carpenter can provide a good living for a family in contemporary America—often better than a white-collar man can provide. Since women choose a standard of living when they marry, they have to take such details into account. As Ernest Burgess and Paul Wallin pointed out long ago,[10] it is men, not women, who tend to be romantic about marriage in our society; the women can't afford to be.

Thus a wife does not leave a blue-collar elite man for trivial reasons. Unless he becomes an alcoholic, or abuses her and the children, she tends to be philosophical about his spending too much time at the tavern. "I wish he would come home from work earlier," one wife said, "but he's a lot better husband than some others I could name."

2. A second strength in these marriages, it seems, is that the wives tend to be from traditional and conservative backgrounds: farms, small towns, and blue-collar families. Thus, their entire life has prepared them to live with the type of man they are married to. It would be difficult to imagine a women's liberationist sustaining a

---

*This woman worked in a small factory on an assembly line.

marriage with any of these men, or any of the men being willing to live with such a woman.

3. A third source of strength in these marriages is the attitude of these men and women toward divorce. Essentially, both sexes in these intact marriages are traditionalists and conservatives, and this in itself tends to prejudice them against divorce. The trend toward divorce did not really begin in the United States until the end of World war I[11] —and even more after World War II—so that the older couples in this group preceded the divorce era.

In addition, the divorced people who patronize a public tavern do not always present the best image of the divorced person in our society; the divorced men often drink excessively, and the divorced women are criticized for "running around," whatever that means.

It is also true that religion is a factor in the attitude of these couples toward divorce. Approximately 60 percent of the regular patrons are nominal members of the Roman Catholic church, while another 15 percent belong to the Lutheran church, which is also conservative in its attitude toward divorce. It is doubtful that the men in this group would be too concerned about what the church thought about divorce, but the women are more sensitive to such influence.

If these men and women are skeptical about the so-called joys of marriage, they are even more skeptical of the virtues of divorce and remarriage.

ARE THESE MARRIAGES SUCCESSFUL?

Students of marriage in modern America would like to have the answer to the following question: Of the marriages that survive in our society, what proportion are functional, that is, meet the needs of the spouses? In one study of middle-age intact marriages by John Cuber and Peggy Haroff,[12] it was concluded that the typical marriage in the sample represented a facade with no substantial marital relationship behind it.

If the test of survival is applied to the intact marriages at The Oasis, they pass with flying colors: they have endured for several decades and appear to be indestructible.

If some test such as "marital satisfaction" were applied, the results would be dubious. Some of the persons in this group would question the concept of "marital satisfaction"—the idea that a man and woman could be married over a long period of time with mutual enjoyment. They could imagine this for short periods of time—a year or two—but they find it difficult to see over a lifetime.

In a very real sense these couples with intact marriages are traditionalists when it comes to marriage: they literally took an oath "for better or worse" and have abided by the agreement. One wife said: "Nobody told me how bad 'worse' could be but then I never asked. I was too anxious to get married to ask any questions."

It is interesting to note that while a majority of the couples married early (before they were twenty) they do not recommend this to their children. They have seen the maturity required by marriage, and they hope that their youngsters will take time to "grow up" before taking the marriage vow.

The language used by couples whose marriages have survived several decades is interesting. The global word *love* is conspicuous by its absence. About the best thing a man can call his wife after thirty-five years of marriage seems to be "a good sport." This usually means that the wife doesn't complain too loudly when the husband does something his wife didn't want him to do—such as buying a new deer rifle when she wanted a davenport.

Some wives refer to their husbands as being "considerate" or "thoughtful" or "good to me and the children." One never hears expressions such as "wonderful" or "terrific"—these are simply not part of the marital vocabulary of middle-aged blue-collar couples.

This same curve of disenchantment applies to almost all of the other aspects of life as these older couples view the world around them.* They no longer hope for peace, or lower taxes, or a cure for cancer—not in their lifetime. They have had too many disappointments to raise their hopes high again. As they have aged they have done what peasants do: they have zeroed in on the indispensable aspects of life: food, drink, good health, sex, a job, children, a house, and recreation. In a sense they might be described as "urban peasants"—farm boys and girls trapped in the city. In this respect they resemble the people Gans described in his book *The Urban Villagers*.

*See chapter 9.

An interesting fact is that these couples are disenchanted in spite of having done quite well in our society: their marriages have survived, the men have good jobs, and so on. One might expect more enthusiasm for the world in such a group, but it is not there.

THE OLDER COUPLES

One of the deficiencies in the research on marriage in our society is the relative absence of longitudinal perspective; we seldom see what happens to married couples over a period of several decades. In the case studies that follow the couples have been married for at least forty years.

"We Never Had an Argument"

"You know, Professor," one of the older wives said to me, "Bob and me have never had an argument in our forty years of marriage.

"That must be a record," I said.

The husband looked at his wife and said: "That's a lot of bullshit—what are you trying to do, feed the Professor a lot of crap?"

The wife stopped talking, resuming her beer drinking, and the husband took over the conversation.

"I'll tell you what, Doc," he said, "marriage is a 50-50 proposition, and people who don't know that better stay single." He drained his beer and ordered another one.

"Now you take this wife of mine—she's a good sport. During the depression when a man could hardly earn a dime, she stuck right by me and saved every penny she could." He paused to light a cigarette.

"Another thing—she always took good care of our kids. If I had a woman that let her kids run around dirty the way some women do I'd kick her right out of the house."

The wife didn't say anything. Then the husband continued.

"Her only trouble is she talks too damn much—and some of the stuff she says don't make sense—like that thing she told you tonight about us never having an argument! Christ Almighty, I wouldn't have a damn woman in the house if I couldn't fight with her once in a while."

The wife was looking in her purse for some snapshots of their grandchildren she wanted to show me.

I looked at the pictures and admired the children—they were handsome.

"A hell of a lot better looking than their grandparents," the husband said.

He turned to his wife. "Come on, mother, Harry says that all grandparents have to be home in bed by 10:30. Let's go!"

The wife protested that she wanted another beer.

"Nope, you've had enough for an old lady"—and out they went.

Golden Wedding Anniversary

"Well, if we both live until next year we will celebrate our golden wedding anniversary."

The speaker was a man in his late seventies. He said his wife was about the same age.

I commented that fifty years of continuous marriage was quite an achievement in a society noted for its high divorce rate.

"I suppose it is," he said, "but we don't think of it that way. When we got married the preacher said it was to be for life and that's the way it's been."

I asked him what he thought the secret of successful marriage was.

"You're the expert on marriage," he said. "You tell me."

I laughed and said I doubted that there were any real "experts" on marriage and that it would be interesting to have the benefit of his long experience.

"Well," he said, "I think that maybe the secret of staying married is to live and let live—to let your partner live his own life as much as possible."

He ordered another beer.

"My wife is smart that way. She realizes that I am a peculiar duck and she lets me go until I get too far out of line. Then we have to have a talk.

"During the depression I didn't have a penny but she never complained. I guess she had married me for 'better or worse' and that was the worst.

"Later on I made a little money and that didn't make any difference to her either."

He said that both he and his wife had endured major medical crises in recent years—cancer and heart attacks.

"But we're still here and we're still together and I guess that's the way it's going to end."

Later on he told us that his two children are both divorced and married for the second time.

I commented that this record was quite different from that of the parents.

"Yes," he said, "it's getting to be a different world. Our boy came into the house one night and said he was leaving his wife—that they couldn't get along. And yet only a few years before that he told us he couldn't live without her. I don't understand it.

"My boy seems very happy with his second wife. She is a fine girl and we think the world of her and the grandchildren."

He said that his daughter also seemed to be happy in her second marriage.

This man grew up on a farm and his philosophy of life seems to stem from this experience. "On the farm it was mostly hard work and we never expected to have much fun. That's why I feel so good about my marriage; it's been better than I expected."

Just Like Brother and Sister

One couple at The Oasis have been married over fifty years and are still less than seventy years old; they married at seventeen and both were in their late sixties when I met them.

It is an interesting and important fact in long marriages that the husband and wife often age at different rates: one of them will look and behave as if they were at least ten years older than the spouse when they are actually about the same age. This was true of this couple: the wife seemed to be at least twenty years older than the husband, whereas in fact only six months separated their birthdays.

I learned later that this man's wife had suffered a severe illness several years earlier that had aged her prematurely. She said very little during the conversation.

Differential aging creates stress in long marriages; if the marriage is to survive the youthful spouse is forced into the role of nurse or caretaker. In some cases I have studied one of the spouses assumes the role of martyr as he or she sacrifices his or her life for the partner.

In the situation of the couple being discussed here the husband had become a nurse-caretaker. He seldom came to The Oasis alone because he did not feel it was wise or desirable to leave his wife in the house by herself any more than was necessary. He did not seem to resent the role of nurse-caretaker.

"You can probably tell that my wife hasn't been well lately," he said. "She had a terrible operation about a year ago and we thought we were going to lose her but she finally pulled through. It was so bad my daughter came home from California to be with us."

We all had another glass of beer, and I asked how long they had been married.

"Oh, God," the husband said, "it's been a helluva long time—over fifty years. We celebrated our golden wedding anniversary two or three years ago."

The wife tried to smile at this point but her illness had apparently affected her ability to change facial expressions and the smile could scarcely be detected.

"Over half a century," the husband said, almost to himself. "We were just kids when we got married—only seventeen years old—and nobody thought we would ever make it. Her parents said we were nuts and my parents said the same thing but they finally gave their permission and here we are."

He turned to his wife, patted her on the cheek, and lit a cigarette for her. She was apparently a chain smoker who could no longer manage a match or a lighter. You could feel the affection that this man still had for his wife after fifty years of marriage. Her attitude toward him at this point in the life cycle was that of the grateful child.

I asked how he accounted for the success of their marriage.

The husband laughed. "It sure as hell wasn't brains," he said, "because we're both dumber than hell. That was one of the reasons why we got married so young—we didn't like school. We thought playing house would be more fun—and it was."

After another round of beer he continued. "You know, Doc, it's a funny thing about a marriage like ours; as the years went by we got more and more alike until we were just like brother and sister. Hell, before my wife's operation people said we even looked alike."

It appeared that as the years had rolled by and the wife's health had failed the husband had gradually taken over the cooking and most of the household management chores.

"Oh, I can cook damn near anything,"* he said, "and it's not bad eating either."

The wife shook her head and tried to smile. The husband laughed.

"Once in a while she complains about the cooking," he said, "but I tell her to be careful or I'll start serving those damn frozen TV dinners. That stops her!"

I asked if their children had married young.

"Hell no!" the husband said. "We made them go through high school—one of them even completed college."

At this point the wife got the pictures of their grandchildren out of her purse. They were handsome, bright-looking kids.

It is always impressive to hear the older married couples at The Oasis talk about their grandchildren. If there is any family role in our society that seem to provide unadulterated joy it appears to be that of grandparent.* It is almost as if these older couples had experienced some disappointment with their children and could now revive the old dreams as they saw the possibilities in their grandchildren.

I bought a round of beer, and the husband said they would have to be heading home. He gently assisted his wife off of her bar stool and they headed for the door. He waved goodnight and she did her best to smile as they disappeared into the night, hand in hand, over fifty years after they had stood up before the minister and had said: "in sickness and in health, for better or worse, until death do us part."

There is something very impressive about meeting an elderly couple like this who have made the marriage vow a bond instead of a travesty.

One can see the cultural change in our society in these older couples as they view the divorces of their children. As they see it, if you really love somebody when you marry them, how can you change your feelings so quickly? It's a good question.

---

*It is amazing how many of the men who frequent The Oasis are competent cooks. It is not unusual to hear them exchange recipes or spend a half hour describing how they prepare a certain specialty.

*The role of grandparent is analyzed in chapter 7.

4 Marital Failure

"She never even said goodbye."
Statement by a deserted man
at The Oasis

INTRODUCTION

In the previous chapter the intact marriages at The Oasis were analyzed. In this chapter the focus will be on the marriages that have failed. In what is probably the most elaborate study of divorce yet published in the United States, William J. Goode concluded that blue-collar workers are unusually prone to marital failure and divorce.[1] Some of the factors related to this will be examined in this chapter. One of the deficiencies of the Goode study was the fact that no husbands were interviewed—only wives were included in the sample. In this chapter the men will be given an opportunity to state their side of the case.

I have been impressed by the variety of divorced men and women one meets at a tavern—they by no means fall into any one category. For this reason an attempt will be made to construct a typology of divorced persons encountered at The Oasis. Divorce is only one form of marital failure and not necessarily the most devastating form; desertion and facade marriage (holy deadlock) can be even more shattering. This matter will also be examined in this chapter.

Divorced men and women in American society have many role problems—sociologically, they are neither single nor married.[2] Massive divorce is so new in our culture that many of the major roles of the divorced person are not adequately defined. This problem will be analyzed in this chapter.

54

Some of the persons in this tavern study seem to have had what might be called a "successful divorce," emerging from it stronger than before, while others have had what might be called an "unsuccessful divorce," learning very little from the experience. What differences can be seen between these two groups? An attempt will be made to illuminate this differential experience with divorce.

A TYPOLOGY OF DIVORCED MEN

It is easy, and not unusual, to think of divorced men as a homogeneous group. One of the interesting findings of this study at The Oasis is that there is a wide range of variation among the divorced men at the tavern. In this section an attempt will be made to sort these men into a set of categories or types.

Men Who Consider Themselves Unsuited for Lifetime Marriage

"How in the hell do you think any woman could stand a guy like me for a lifetime?"

The speaker was a man in his fifties, now in his third marriage.

"My first wife stood it for seven years and then gave me up as a hopeless case. She married me to reform me—to make a nice boy out of me—and it didn't work."

He paused to have another shot of brandy. "Hell, I could have told her the plan to reform me wouldn't work if she had told me that was what she had in mind."

He waved to the bartender. "Harry!" he shouted, "give me another shot of that golden juice—I'm feeling better and better. And give The Professor here a glass of beer—he seems to be pretty decent for a professor."

Then he went on. "My second wife was a damn good woman—she realized it was hopeless to try and change Old Charlie. She just ignored my bad points and enjoyed the good parts. I really loved that woman and then she died."

Another shot of brandy and another cigarette. "This third wife and I get along pretty good. We fight like hell about once a week and that seems to clear the air. When I get too far out of line she belts me one—and don't ever think she can't punch. That girl packs a hell of a wallop. But she's a nice kid and we get along pretty good."

Just for fun I asked Charlie if he felt that after three marriages he understood women.

"Dammit, Doc," he snorted, "questions like that are what drive a man to drink." He ordered another shot of brandy, downed it in one gulp (with no chaser), and wiped his lips. "By God, that is good stuff," he said.

Then he turned to me. "Understand women? Me? Hell, no. I gave that up thirty years ago when I was married to my first wife. Now I don't worry about whether I understand them—the main question is whether they understand *me*."

At this point an elderly lady that Old Charlie knew entered the tavern, and he took off to dance with her (somebody had begun playing a polka on the juke box). When I left to go home a half hour later Old Charlie was whirling around the bar, dancing with one woman after another.

One night, several months later, Charlie and his wife had one of their famous fights at the bar. Charlie had consumed more brandy than usual and either said something or did something that was too much for his wife. She began to curse him and he replied in kind. Finally she punched him in the jaw, knocking him off of his bar stool. He got up, put on his hat, took the car, and went home. Later on, his wife hitched a ride home with another couple.

The amazing thing about the fight was that the next morning (a Saturday) Charlie and his wife were sitting at the bar as if nothing had happened the night before.

Later on I asked the proprietor about this. "They are very much in love," he said. "I have known them for fifteen years and they have a good marriage. That is just their way of expressing their feelings."

You would have to know Old Charlie to understand the truth of what he says about marriage. He is such a wild character, so completely untamed, that only a very unique woman could live with him successfully. He insists on a woman taking him as he is: "I don't want them to reform me," he states. And yet, as he says, there is a lot of good in him to love if a woman can only see it. This is demonstrated by the many good friends he has at The Oasis. Charlie

is "marriageable," whereas some of the divorced men at The Oasis
are not (see below).

Men Who Have Tried Marriage and Don't Care for It

The next man is somewhat similar to the one above—he is a wild
character—but he differs in that he never had any desire to remarry
after his first divorce.

"Me and marriage don't mix, Doc. I tried it once but it was like
being in a damn prison. Hell, she wanted me to sit home at night
with her and *watch television!* What a hell of a way to waste a night
when a man could be drinking or shooting pool or playing cards or
going to a baseball game. I don't want no part of it. Not me!"

The speaker was a man often called The Wild Irishman at the
tavern.

"Oh, hell," he said. "It may be all right for some guys—and if we
had had any kids I would have tried to stick it out. But it didn't
seem to suit me very well—too confining."

This man lives in a very comfortable mobile home, has an excellent
job in the construction industry, and seems to be very happy. As a
rule he limits his heavy drinking to weekends. He has a girl friend
that he usually refers to as The Queen. He seems to be fond of this
woman but one has the feeling that he will never marry again. You
get the impression that a man like this would have "gone west" if he
had lived in the days of Daniel Boone. There is a fierce sort of
independence about him—perhaps it is because he is Irish—that a
woman would have to understand and accept if she were to live with
him successfully.

"I got caught once," he will say, "but The Irishman don't plan to
put his paw in that trap again."

A man such as this loves sports more than he probably can love a
woman. He is one of the few old-time baseball fans who can tell you
how many games Walter Johnson won in any particular year. His
team is the Chicago Cubs, and he makes frequent pilgrimages to
worship at the shrine. As this is being written the Cubs are having a
good year, and you can see it in The Wild Irishman's face.

He is also a great football fan—both high school and professional.

He follows his old high school team and goes home to watch them play whenever possible. This is unusual in a man in his late forties or early fifties who no longer lives in his home community.

In the summer and fall The Irishman attends country fairs because he loves harness horse racing. On occasion he may journey to Chicago to watch the horses run.

He is a good pool player and would probably rather shoot pool than eat (and nobody has ever accused him of not enjoying his food). He also enjoys a card game if the stakes are right.

He is a gambler—he will bet on anything at any time, and for almost any amount.

A frustrated and disappointed wife might accuse a man like this of being irresponsible, but a cursory review of his occupational history disproves such a charge. He has operated at least two businesses successfully and presently holds a construction job that involves about as much responsibility as a blue-collar worker can be assigned. The key values in The Wild Irishman's life are independence and freedom—values that are not maximized in the American system of marriage.

At first glance Old Charlie and The Wild Irishman may seem quite similar in that neither one of them can imagine himself married to one woman for a lifetime, but the differences between the two men are substantial: Old Charlie does not enjoy being a bachelor; to him marriage is a vital part of life. He doesn't feel that any one woman could last a lifetime with him, but the solution is to find another woman. For The Wild Irishman, a bachelor life-style, with a steady girl friend, seems to be more congenial. These men (a) like women, and (b) do not blame their wives for their marital failure.

The Woman Haters

The men in this group have tried marriage and discovered that they don't really like women as a species: they are really "woman haters." They are quite different from the two men above, both of whom enjoy women but find marriage "difficult."

One man is now about sixty years old. He was once married, thirty-five years ago, for a few months and has never seriously considered remarriage. He lives alone and has not had a "girl friend" for many years. Except for his mother and sister (both deceased) he seldom has a good word for any member of the opposite sex.

One day this man said:

"I bet you think I have never been married."

I admitted that my impression was that he had always been a happy bachelor, as he seemed to be now.

"That ain't true," he said. "I was married once thirty-five years ago and by God I'm glad I got out of it when I did. She was no damn good, that woman."

I asked him what had happened.

"What happened? Lee, look, I used to come home from work and find she hadn't even gotten dressed yet—still in her bathrobe. The apartment would be dirty and not even any supper on the stove!

"One day I came home and found things in a mess and I said to her—'you lazy bitch, get your clothes and get the hell out of here!'

"She left that night and I never saw her again. Since then I met several women who wanted to get married but not me again. I can't see it."

He explained that no children had been involved and the marriage had apparently lasted only a few months.

The amazing thing is that this man ever married at all. Those who know him feel that he is the perfect bachelor type: he likes to cook, seems to enjoy keeping his apartment neat and clean, and is extremely independent. One can hardly imagine him married to anybody in his present state, but of course he might have been somewhat different thirty-five years ago.

"My Wife Was a 'Bad' Woman"

These men are relatively numerous at The Oasis. Some of them have been married (and divorced) more than once. They are not "woman haters," nor do they consider themselves unsuited for marriage. They tend to feel that they picked the wrong woman but plan to marry again—if they have not already done so.

"My first wife was nuts," one man said. "She must have cost me $25,000 in doctor's bills. I finally took her to a psychiatrist and he told me what was wrong with her. I got a divorce after that."

"How is your second marriage working out?"

"Seems to be OK so far."

Another man in this category said:

'I wrote a check one day and it bounced. When I called the bank they said my wife had been in that morning and had taken all of the money out of our checking account—almost $500.

"Christ! Was I mad! I found out later she had given the money to her goddamn mother.

"I packed her clothes and left them on her mother's porch and went to see a lawyer about a divorce."

There were no children involved in this marriage. This man says that his second marriage, which has survived for over thirty-five years, has been "very happy."

"My first wife was crazy," he says. "She died not long after our divorce and I sometimes think she had a brain tumor or something."

The next man feels that he got a "raw deal" from his ex-wife.

"Doc," he said, "if you ever write that damn book, put this one in. It should scare the hell out of any single guys who ever see the book."

This man's story is that he was financially "rooked" by his first wife.

"Look," he said, "we owned these two duplex apartment houses— that is, the bank and us owned them together. My wife collected the rents and was supposed to be making the payments on the damn mortgage.

"One day I got a notice from the bank that we were behind in our payments. When I asked her why, she said some of the people hadn't paid their rent. Later on I found out that she had collected the rents but had kept the money and hadn't paid the bank.

"Before I could get all the legal separation papers drawn up she used every charge account we had in town—dresses, coats, shoes, everything. And you know what else? She even ran up a $300 telephone bill on me, calling up her mother and all her damn relatives.

"I figure that dame took me for $16,000. I was five years paying all those bills."

This man is a skilled mechanic who earns good money and was apparently on his way to financial security until his marriage failed. He has not remarried but has a "steady" girl friend.

The last man in this category was a professional musician at one time, playing all over the United States in country and western-style bands. He is now a blue-collar worker.

"I was married twice," he once said, "but both of my woman 'went bad.' I guess traveling the way I did they got lonesome and some other guy stepped right in."

He is now a bachelor.

"Would you like to get married again?"

'I would if I could find me a good woman but I'm sort of afraid. When you get burned twice you get to be more careful."

The men in this group like the idea of marriage, and they like women. Their problem, as they see it, is "to find me a good woman."

Divorced Men with Personality Problems

Whether the men in this category recognize it or not, the other regular patrons at The Oasis consider them to have personality problems that would make marriage with them impossible. As one woman at the tavern put it, "I wouldn't marry any of those guys for a million bucks. It wouldn't be worth it."

All of these men drink "too much." It is not clear whether the excessive drinking preceeded their marital problems or developed later.

The problem, however, is not just that they drink large amounts of beer and/or liquor—many of the successfully married men at The Oasis drink "too much"—but the men in this category are not "lovable" when they are "fried" or "have a snootful." These men become abusive and/or very difficult when intoxicated. They may spend their entire week's wages at taverns, stay out all night, go out with other women, or go home and mistreat their wife and children. Sooner or later the wife can't take it any longer and files for divorce. Several reconciliations may follow but eventually the marriage is ended.

One of these men refers to himself as a "two-time loser."

"You probably know that I am now in the middle of my second divorce," one of the regular customers said. "I keep looking for a woman like my mother—as *good* as my mother was—but I can't find one.

"I finally told my first wife, 'for God's sake quit trying to be like my mother because you'll never make it—not on the best day of your life.' "

This man apparently served in the armed forces for over twenty years in many parts of the world. He is still handsome.

"Look, Doc," he said, "marriage doesn't have much to do with sex. Hell, a man today can have that whenever and wherever he wants it. It's the goddamn loneliness that makes a man commit marriage. He wants somebody he can love, somebody to come home to—and by God I can't find that person."

He took a few gulps of his beer and went on.

"My trouble is that I'm not a good bachelor—I hate making the goddamn beds and washing the goddamn dishes—and yet I'm not a good husband."

After a while he said: "What do you think is wrong with me, Doc?"

I suggested that perhaps he had loved his mother too much.

He gave me a queer look of disbelief and then said: "How in the hell can a man love his mother too much? I always thought the more love a child had for his parents the better off he was."

I said that some psychiatrists wrote about men with a "mother complex" and that maybe this was part of his problem. This comment riled him up (he was also beginning to feel the four bottles of beer he had now consumed).

"Those goddamn headshrinkers!" he exclaimed. "What the hell do they know? I went to one of them when my first wife and I were separated while I was stationed in Germany. He kept asking me about my dreams and all that crap—he seemed like a fairy to me. I went twice and never went back."

Many of the divorced men who frequent The Oasis are bitter about some aspect of their divorce—and children often figure in this bitterness. This veteran of over twenty years in the armed forces was no exception.

"You know what my first wife did, Doc? She wouldn't let me visit my son—she kept using all kinds of excuses to keep us apart. I finally smuggled an airline ticket to the kid and he flew down to see me." He ordered another beer.

"You know what happened? The next day she and her second husband came down with a goddamn lawyer and had me charged with *kidnapping!*

"How in the hell can you kidnap your own kid?"

I said that the courts seemed to have no difficulty with this dilemma; several estranged parents had been charged with kidnapping their own children in Wisconsin in recent years.

This man, when sober, is one of the most handsome and charming men who frequent The Oasis. When he drinks too much, however, his personality undergoes almost a complete change, and at that point he and women become incompatible. As he says: "I can't live with them and I can't live without them"

The next man's personality does not change when he drinks—the problem is that he is seldom sober. Although he is well liked at the tavern none of the women there consider him marriage material. As one of them observed: "he is married to the bottle."

"What happened to my marriage? You tell me. I don't know. All I know is that I came home from work one night and she was gone—and left the kids for me to take care of."

He ordered another glass of beer. "I have never even had a postcard from her. And when she left she didn't even say goodbye."

"What do you think happened to the marriage?"

"I don't know. Maybe I drank too much once in a while but lots of guys in here do that and their wives don't leave them. I can't figure it out."

Another man who has been divorced twice made this statement:

"Women? Piss on them. When my second wife had me jailed for what she called 'nonsupport' that was the end of the line for me. From now on my motto is 'screw 'em and leave 'em,' and that's what they deserve."

This man drinks heavily; spends a great deal of time in various taverns, and appears to have affairs with numerous women. It is difficult to imagine him successfully married to any one woman.

Teenage Marriages That End in Divorce

The last category of divorced men represent the type of person who married quite young, was divorced young, and then achieved success in his second marriage. These men do not exhibit any particular personality problems, nor are they bitter about divorce. Here is an example:

"There's no mystery about my divorce," one regular patron said to me. "I was just a young punk who thought sex was the only important thing in life and I figured you could get more sex married than you could single—a point I am not so sure about today.

"My parents urged me not to get married and to go on to college but I wouldn't listen. Three years later I was a father who no longer loved his wife. I realize now that I was in love with sex, not this particular woman."

After a pause he smiled and said: "Don't get me wrong, Doc. I haven't changed my mind about sex, but I have learned a lot about marriage and love since my first marriage."

This man is now married, has several children, and seems to be quite happy in his second marriage. His main regret about his first marriage seems to be that it kept him from going to college, which in turn has been a serious problem in his attempts to move up in the occupational structure. He earns a good living but feels that he could have gone much further if he had had more formal education.

This man has no bitterness toward his former wife; he feels they were both too young to know what they were doing.

In concluding this analysis of the divorced men at The Oasis the most impressive fact, to me, is the range of variation in these men. About all they have in common is the fact that they are divorced.

Now let us look at the divorced women at the tavern.

THE DIVORCED WOMEN

The divorced women at The Oasis are also impressive in their variety. Some of them still regard marriage as the only way of life for an adult female; some continue to love the opposite sex while others are bitter; some seem to have emerged from their marital failure strong and posed while others appear defeated and permanently damaged. It is important that divorced women not be stuffed into one vast pigeon-hole as if they were all alike. The purpose of this section is to demonstrate the amazing variety of this group.

"I Don't Know How You Can Compete with Those German Gals"

In this case the divorced woman had been married to a career man in the armed forces. When she was permitted to join him overseas she discovered that the marriage was "all washed up."

"After World War II my first husband was sent to Germany as part of the occupation forces," she said. "After he had been there several months, housing for families became available and he was authorized to bring his dependents.

"Well, I got the furniture crated up, took the kids out of school, and off we flew to Germany.

"At first things seemed to be going pretty well. Everything was cheap, our house was not too bad, and the armed forces operated a good school for American kids."

She stopped to light another cigarette. "But then things started to happen. He came home one day and said he had to go to another city for a week's temporary duty. At the time I didn't suspect anything but I found out later that this was a damn lie—he spent the whole week in Nuremberg, where we were stationed, shacking up with this German babe.

"Later on he would come home and say he had to stand duty all night—one or two nights a week.

"I finally became suspicious that all was not well and went to see his superior officer. I then discovered that the week's temporary duty and all of the night duty were a myth—none of it was true. All of that time he had spent with this German gal.

"When I confronted him with what I had found out, he admitted that the affair with this German woman had begun before me and the kids ever got to Germany.

"I asked him what he wanted to do and he said he guessed he was in love with the *fraulein*.

"That was enough for me. I had the furniture crated again, took the kids out of school, and back we flew to the good old U.S.A."

After a pause she said: "It's a hell of a feeling to find yourself deserted in a strange country thousands of miles from home."

"Did he ever marry the German girl?" I asked.

"I don't know and I don't care," she said. "Those German women were so hungry for men they would do anything—American women just can't compete with them. They look up to a man as if he was God—and American women don't see it that way."

This woman has now remarried and seems to be quite happy.

A Wartime Romance

In the next case the marital failure is described as a typical World War II romance that ended in marriage and then divorce.

"Well, you don't need any computer to find out what caused my divorce. I was working away from home during World War II and met a lonely soldier. He seemed like a pretty decent sort of guy and we had a nice brief wartime romance."

The woman speaking is now sixty or so and she was talking about her one and only marriage.

"I guess I was as lonely as he was, to tell the truth.

"Anyhow, we got married one Saturday, had a few weeks together, and then he went overseas."

She paused to drink some of her beer.

"After the war there didn't seem to be any use carrying on—there didn't seem to be anything between us. Since we didn't have any kids we decided to call it quits."

After a pause she said: "Don't you think I did my part to help the morale of the armed forces?"

She was asked if she had ever remarried.

"No. I've been single for almost thirty-five years now."

"Why didn't you ever marry again?"

"It's very simple—nobody asked me."

"Would you like to get married again?"

'If I found the right man and he thought I was the right woman."

There seemed to be no bitterness or any feeling of failure in this woman, only a sort of nostalgic melancholy as she resurrected the memories from long ago.

"I Should Never Have Gotten Married"

The speaker is a woman approaching thirty. She has been divorced once and is now living with a man. She says that she no longer believes in marriage as a way of life.

"I should never have gotten married. I was pregnant and wanted to have an abortion but my parents talked me out of it. They talked about sin and all of that crap. Now I have a baby and have left my husband. It's a hell of a mess."

I asked why she no longer believes in marriage.

"For the same reason that I no longer believe in God or chastity or any of that stuff. I want to enjoy myself, not do things because somebody else wants me to do them."

Her attitude toward marriage does not reflect any bitterness toward her former husband. "He's not a bad guy. We had plenty of sex and he was always good to me—but I don't like being restricted to one man—I like MEN period."

This young woman feels that girls are brainwashed into thinking that marriage is the only way of life for women. "When you're a little kid they start giving you dolls and baby clothes and that's the whole pitch—go out and find a man, get married, have kids, and take care of your house. You are never allowed to see that some women shouldn't get married. And then after you get married you begin to realize that something is wrong. But by then it's too late."

This woman regards herself as "liberated"—she has revolted against her middle-class parents and has moved into the blue-collar world. She says she would like to be sterilized and to avoid any permanent arrangements with men in the future.

The other women at The Oasis consider this young woman as being "sick." The men at the tavern regard her as "wild." She is a threat to both sexes in that she rejects much of what they believe about marriage and parenthood.

"I Don't Believe in Marriage Anymore"

This woman was a fringe member of The Oasis group—she was not accepted by the other women at the tavern. At one time she must have been quite beautiful, but many years of frustration and despair had taken their toll. In recent years she had been hospitalized for mental illness and alcoholism, and her children had been placed in foster homes by the state welfare department.

"I don't believe in marriage any more," she once remarked. "Luke and I aren't married—we're just living together. I guess the men in here call it 'shacking up.'

"I was married once, though," she continued, "to a big handsome bruiser who got me pregnant. He was the first guy I ever slept with."

She stopped to buy a pack of cigarettes and order another beer.

"Anyhow," she continued, "this guy left me for another woman and I ended up in Mendota.* Later on the judge took my children away from me and put them in foster homes." She looked in her purse for some snapshots of her two children, a girl and a boy.

"Don't you think they're handsome?"

I said that they certainly were.

"I saw them three years ago but then I went to Mendota again and I haven't seen them since."

"Did you ever remarry after your divorce?"

"No, I was afraid to. I was working in a restaurant and met this foreign student who had lots of money and I lived with him for two years—or maybe it was three."

She ordered another beer.

"Anyhow, this foreign student was real nice. He had this beautiful foreign car and we would roar over to Milwaukee or down to Chicago for dinner at some expensive place."

Another beer. "He bought me some nice clothes—in fact he got me this dress I have on. Do you like it?"

"It's very pretty."

After a pause I asked her what happened to the foreign student.

"Oh, he finished his degree and went back to Egypt or Iran or someplace like that. I wanted him to take me along but he said his father was a big wheel over there and would never approve of him having an American woman."

Later on she said: "I used to be pretty. Do you think I'm pretty now?"

"You look pretty good for what you've been through," I said.

She said that after the foreign student left she went back to work as a waitress and that was how she met Luke, the man she was living with now.

"It wasn't a very fancy place, sort of a truck stop, and he walked in one day. I've been with him a year now. Don't know how long it will last."

After another round of beer she said:

"Would you like to shoot a game of pool? I learned out at Mendota. They were real nice to me there."

*This is the state mental hospital serving this area.

We adjourned to the pool table and shot a game of eight ball.

It would appear that this woman has never been able to stabilize her relationships with men. At one time, when she was younger and more attractive, she apparently associated with men who were affluent; her original husband, she claims, owned a cocktail lounge where she had been employed as a waitress. At the time of this interview she had worked her way down to the bottom of the social class ladder; Luke had an uncertain income and the two were living in a rundown house at the edge of the village.

This woman has no trouble meeting and attracting men. Her problems are (a) she can't pick out a "good man," and (b) she can't stick to one man.

Her mental illness appears to be a mild form of schizophrenia complicated by alcoholism. One has the impression that she will never be any better than she is now, and will probably get worse.

After a few months this woman disappeared from The Oasis, not to be seen again.

Divorce Was the End of the Line

Some people seem to never recover from the failure of a marriage. Their life appears to have been so intimately interwoven with the married partner that they can never reassemble the pieces after the broken love affair is ended. A woman who frequented The Oasis seems to fit into this category.

This person, in her forties, had been married for twenty years when her husband asked for a divorce. "He said he had met another woman," she said. "I tried to talk him out of it with no luck."

After her divorce this woman began to drink excessively, neglected her children, and associated with men who were fringe members of the tavern: men who were usually unemployed, who drank excessively, and in general were not accepted by the tavern regulars.

Eventually, this woman was admitted to the state mental hospital in the area for treatment of alcoholism. Her children were removed from the home and placed in foster homes by the welfare authorities.

Upon release from the mental hospital this woman resumed her excessive drinking and was finally evicted from her apartment. Being unable to find another place to live she began to live (if that is the word for it) in her car in the parking lot of the tavern. She would stay at the bar until the 1 A.M. closing time, use the restroom facilities, and retire to her car for the night. In the morning, when the tavern opened, she would use the washroom facilities and take her place at the bar. Her clothes and a few other possessions could be seen stored in the rear seat of her car.

After about a week or ten days of the above routine this woman disappeared from The Oasis. In a few months it was reported by one of the customers that she had died in a nearby state.

This case has some similarities with the preceding one but in the former case the woman was able to survive by going from one man to another, even though she was deteriorating gradually. In the present case the woman was never able to replace her husband with any sort of stable male companion. She once said: "I think all men are liars. I don't trust them any more."

Discussion of the Divorced Women

The writer feels that the divorced women at The Oasis, like the men, are impressive in their variety. Some are strong, stable persons who made an unfortunate marriage, divorced, and seem to be successfully remarried. These women hold responsible jobs, rear their children, and drink moderately. They feel that their marital failure was the result of marrying "the wrong man."

Another group of divorced women, however, seem to represent a different set of circumstances: some appear to have deep-seated personality problems, others do not accept the marital system as it is presently organized, while others do not seem to be able to find "the right man."

It is my belief that observers of the divorce scene in America have failed adequately to reflect the variety of the divorced men and women in our society. It is hoped that this might be one of the contributions of this study.

ROLE PROBLEMS OF DIVORCED MEN

Many observers have pointed out that the position of the divorced person in American society is not an easy one: their status tends to be ambiguous and their social roles not clearly defined.[3] The major role problems of the divorced men seem to be the following:

The Financial Role

A considerable percentage of these men have financial problems; they are required by law to support the wife and children from their previous marriage, yet they have to provide for their own needs and if remarried have to support two families. Some of the men have been arrested for nonsupport at some point after their divorce and some of the others are delinquent in support payments.[4]

The economic problems of the divorced man are very real: a decent apartment will cost at least $125 a month; he has to have a car; he is usually involved with at least one woman and this costs money; his food bill is high because he often eats out; his liquor expenditures are higher than average because he hates to be alone in his apartment and tends to spend more time than most people in bars and taverns. One does not hear married men at The Oasis complain about money problems but divorced men are quite vocal about theirs.

Parental Role Problems

When his divorce was first obtained, or when the original separation took place, the divorced man, as a rule, expected to continue his role as father of his children. His decision to leave their mother (if it was his decision) did not include the idea of abandoning his children. He will tell you that he still loves his kids but he no longer loves his wife.

But these plans often do not work out. The wife acquires a new boy friend (or a new husband) and when the former husband wants to see his children the new man is usually around the place. Another fact is that the divorced man is prone to move to a new community, which places distance between him and his children.

Many of the divorced men feel guilty about their inability to continue properly their role as father. A carpet installer put it this way: "I drove all the way from Las Vegas just to see my kids. Hell, I wouldn't drive across the street to see my ex-wife." This man said that the only thing he regretted about his divorce was the separation it had created between him and his children.

There is no easy solution to this parental problem for the divorced man. It is one of the costs of marital failure that he had not fully anticipated.

The Affectional Role

In Hunt's study of the divorced person in our society, cited above, he concluded that loneliness—the loss of the love object—is the outstanding characteristic of these men and women. Sex is no problem for most divorced men (or women). In an urban society sex is readily available for almost any man who will go out and look for it. His real problem is *love;* he needs somebody who cares for him and is emotionally close to him. This is a lot harder to find than sex. One divorced man said: "There is lots of screwing available around these parts but it sure gets lonely back in that apartment."

On the tavern juke box one of the favorite songs says "hello, walls" as a divorced or separated man looks around his living quarters.

The divorced man tries to solve this psychic loss problem by getting a steady girl friend, or by moving in with his girl friend, or by a new marriage. It is literally true in our society that the only cure for a broken love affair is a new love affair. Americans are not reared to live alone and like it.

ROLE PROBLEMS OF DIVORCED WOMEN

Economic Role

In the Goode study, cited earlier, the divorced women complained about their financial problems. The problem of nonsupport by divorced men has reached epidemic proportions in the United States. One noon at The Oasis a young boy was displaying proudly a dollar bill that he said had been given to him by his father. The mother, a divorced person, turned to the other persons at the bar and said: "Yeah, his daddy gave him the dollar but his daddy is also $4000 behind in his support payments."

Even though a divorced mother may have a reasonable support payment agreement with her former husband she can never be sure in any given month that the check will arrive. One woman said:

"Would you believe that last year the one month he missed was December—with all of the kids just dying to see what Santa would bring them for Xmas?" She managed to survive the emergency by borrowing from her parents.

Part of the problem here, discussed earlier, is that the divorced man himself is often unable to meet his various financial commitments. If he has very much hostility toward his former wife he may derive some pleasure from skipping a check once in a while. One divorced man said: "I went all the way to Hong Kong to work so my wife couldn't collect money from my wages."

Many divorced women find that they have to seek outside employment to balance their budget. But this creates other problems, as we shall see in the next section.

Role Conflicts of the Employed Divorced Woman

An outside job has many advantages for the divorced woman: it gives her a chance to meet men, one of whom might turn out to be her future husband; she will also meet other women, some of whom have problems similar to hers; it helps to solve her financial problems; and, finally, if she has young children a job gives the mother some time away from the children so that she can enjoy them more when she is at home.

If a divorced woman has young children, however, an outside job may create certain role conflicts: if she is unable to obtain (or afford) good care for her children when she is out of the home, neighbors and relatives may accuse her of "neglecting" her children; the hours of employment often do not coincide with school hours or other situations when the children need their mother at the same time that her employer needs her (childhood illnesses are a good example of this conflict).

A divorced mother at The Oasis described the above problems in this way:

"Last week the store where I work had a big sale on and the manager wanted me to work every evening. My baby-sitter could only come over three nights so I had to ask my sister to help out the other two nights.

"During the school year I don't get off work until 5:30 in the evening but school is out at 3:30. The kids are not allowed to play at the school once classes are over so I have to have somebody at home to take care of them until I get home." This woman added that she liked to work outside of the home but that proper care of her children presented many problems when she had a job.

Role Conflicts Related to Dating

Sooner or later most divorced women hope to remarry. They may not indicate this openly but the vast majority (at least 80 percent) do marry again eventually. These women realize that you don't meet your next husband sitting at home watching television with the children. You have to get out and circulate if you are to meet men. When they do meet a man who may interest them—perhaps only as a temporary dating partner—very real problems arise if they have young children. How many evenings a week can such a mother go out with her boy friend? How late can she stay out with a baby-sitter at home with the children? How late can the boy friend stay at her house? Can he stay overnight at her place? Can she stay over-night at his place? How much will people "talk" if she is not careful of her behavior during this period? Will her children be upset by the appearance of a new man on the scene? All of these are very real questions for the divorced woman with young children (or adolescent children).

MARITAL FAILURE OTHER THAN DIVORCE

Most of the concern about marital failure in our society seems to be with divorce—at least one gets this impression from the mass media and textbooks on marriage and the family. Watching and listening to persons at The Oasis who are experiencing marital failure have made me wonder whether, indeed, there are not forms of marital failure worse than divorce. Desertion would be a good illustration of the point I am trying to make.

One of the most traumatized persons at the tavern who experienced marital failure during the period of this study was a man in his late forties who returned home one evening to find a note from his wife that she had gone to California with another man. The wife left three minor children at home when she departed, with no plans for their supervision or care. The man went into a state of depression and attempted to cure this problem by extensive use of alcohol. He would sometimes bring his children to the tavern while he engaged in his prolonged drinking bouts (a practice not approved of by the proprietor). In talking about his experience this man said: "She never even said goodbye. What a hell of a way to end a marriage after twenty-five years." This man deteriorated markedly and did not recover until he met a widow and developed a significant relationship with her.

Another man at the tavern was also deserted by his wife during the period of this study. This woman also left town with another man, but in this case the wife decided she had made a mistake and asked her husband to take her back. He was very much in love with her and was glad to have her return.

The impressive part of the above situation was the drastic decline in the man when his wife deserted him. He could not eat; he lost weight; and his friends were afraid he might commit suicide. After his wife returned he recovered rapidly.

A woman at the tavern sometimes called The Blonde Bomber claims she was deserted by her first husband (since then she has lived with a series of men). In her conversation one gets the impression that she has never recovered from the trauma of her first marital failure.

There are several features of desertion that could make it more traumatic than divorce: (1) the action is unilateral (one spouse decides to end the marriage) whereas most divorces seem to represent a bilateral decision by the couple; (2) unlike divorce there is no court supervision of desertion, so that important decisions such as custody of the children, child support, and visitation rights have not been settled; (3) the deserted person, unlike the divorced person, is not free to marry unless he or she takes steps to dissolve the marriage—which means that these persons often live with their next lover instead of getting married; and (4) the psychological impact of desertion seems to me to be greater than that in divorce, perhaps because the action to desert is unilateral and also because the blow seems to be unexpected by the spouse deserted.

Another type of marital failure that may be more destructive than divorce is what I have called holy deadlock: facade marriages that have never been terminated.[5] One couple who represented this form of marital failure used to come into the tavern and sit at opposite ends of the bar. They would spend the entire evening in this fashion, never exchanging a word. Usually they would both become intoxicated by about eleven in the evening and then leave together. One night the police had to be called because this couple were fighting in the parking lot. They were both quite large persons, and the wife seemed to be winning the fight when the police broke it up. On one occasion the man was heard to refer to his wife as "that damn whore at the other end of the bar." It seems reasonable to assume that a "marriage" of this type would be more destructive than divorce.

In another marriage that seemed to represent holy deadlock the wife would sit at the bar and ridicule her husband. "Look at that dumb shit-ass," she said one night, "he thinks he is so damn smart. Hell, he doesn't even know his ass from a hole in the ground."

On another occasion she made fun of her husband's sexual ability: "He can't even cut the mustard any more," she said. Her husband slapped her in the face and left the tavern when she made this remark. This couple have been married for thirty-five years and have several grown children. Who can imagine what their life is like at home if it is that destructive in public?

After one of the above displays a married woman at the bar commented: "Why don't those dumb bastards separate or get a divorce? They are tearing each other apart."

In one other instance of facade marriage a man whose wife never came to the tavern would constantly disparage her to the customers at the bar.

"I had a horrible experience this morning, Doc," this man once said to me.

"What happened?"

"I woke up in bed beside my wife—Christ! was that a shock."

This man would then procede to tell how homely his wife was and how attractive the various women were that he was sleeping with. The other customers at the bar found this man disgusting.

There are several reasons why a facade or depleted marriage that is not terminated may be more destructive than divorce:[6] (1) there is no end to the war—the couple continue to live together and continue to damage each other; (2) unlike divorced persons the facade couples are not really free to find another love object who might meet their needs; they may have affairs, of course, but this is usually not the same as a successful remarriage; (3) these facade couples are in essence living a lie: they are pretending to the public that they have a "marriage" when in fact they have only a piece of paper that says they were once married in the eyes of the law. But what they really have is a dead marriage that they have refused to bury. The divorced persons at The Oasis feel sorry for these facade couples—they certainly do not envy them.

THE CONCEPT OF A SUCCESSFUL DIVORCE

Most Americans are used to thinking of divorce as an unqualified disaster. Mel Krantzler, in his book *Creative Divorce*,[7] argues that this is not necessarily the case—he has developed the concept of a *successful* divorce.

Krantzler takes the position that divorce can be successful when:

1. It leads to growth in the person who does not just blame his previous spouse for his problems but examines his own contribution to the death of the marriage.
2. The individual takes a good look at his (or her) life-style and values to see what might be improved.
3. The question is asked: is marriage a viable way of life for me?
4. If remarriage emerges from the above process as a desirable goal, then caution is exercised in choosing a new marital partner.

Several of the men and women at The Oasis seem to have had a successful divorce in the above sense: some learned that marriage was not for them; others learned enough from the failure of their first marriage to achieve satisfaction in their second one.

Other men and women at The Oasis appear to have learned very little, if anything, from their divorce. These people seem to like being married but can't adjust to living successfully with any particular partner. One generic characteristic of these men and women seems to be their willingness to blame their marital failure on their spouse. It would be helpful if researchers in the field of marital failure would attempt to isolate the differences between the successfully divorced and the unsuccessfully divorced. To date this does not seem to appear in the literature.

THE TAVERN AS A RESOURCE FOR REMARRIAGE

Some persons may regard the tavern as a poor place in which to find a husband, but during the period of this study I was able to identify three women who met their second husbands at The Oasis. For the most part they felt that the tavern had been very useful to them in their effort to remarry. "When my husband died," one widow said, "I just stayed at home nursing my sorrow. Then one night I came down here with a girl friend and we had a good time. Eventually I met the man I'm married to now."

She felt that the tavern was a good place to meet men if you were "selective" in choosing your dates. "Sure, all the married men would like to go out with a young widow and relieve her sorrow (as they put it), but I never dated any of those guys. I finally met a nice man whose wife had died and who was as lonely as I was. That's the one I married."

A divorced woman walked across the street to The Oasis from a laundromat one afternoon and met a divorced man who eventually became her second husband.

"I had seen this tavern near the laundromat but never had enough nerve to come in by myself. This day it was hot and I decided to slip over for a cold beer while the clothes were in the dryer.

"It didn't seem like a bad place—the proprietor was very pleasant to me—and I started stopping in once a week or so in the evening." She met a divorced man at the tavern who is now her second husband. "I think he is a real nice guy," she said. Their marriage appears to be successful.

In the third situation the proprietor introduced a male customer whose wife had died to a widow who had moved into the community and who stopped in at The Oasis from time to time. This couple eventually married and held their wedding reception at the tavern.

This remarriage seems to have had dubious results, and Harry (the proprietor) was not sure he should have arranged their first meeting.

"I am retiring from the match-making field," he told me. "I don't think they were suited for each other."

While statistics are not available, it seems likely that a substantial percentage of divorced and widowed persons meet their new marital partner in taverns and other public drinking places. This, then, appears to be one of the functions of such establishments.

5 Battle of the Sexes

"Women are so goddamm sneaky."
Statement by a man at The Oasis

INTRODUCTION

In any society one of the functional imperatives is to evolve some system whereby the two sexes can work together effectively. It is my belief that this has not been accomplished in the blue-collar group covered in this study.[1]

In an earlier examination of blue-collar marriages, Lee Rainwater came to this conclusion: "Working class men, even more than men in general, tend to think of women as temperamental, emotional, demanding, and irrational; they are sometimes in deadly earnest when they, with the hero of *My Fair Lady,* ask with exasperation, 'Why can't a woman be more like a man?' They think that women do silly things: They cry for no reason, they argue in petty ways about the things a man wants to do, and they are always acting hurt for no apparent reason."[2] Some of these attitudes were found in this study and will be examined in this chapter—as will the ideas the women at The Oasis have concerning men.

This discussion is limited to generic items—males and females looking at each other as two different species. How for example, does women's liberation look at the level of the blue-collar aristocrat? Are blue-collar men and women suffering from differential social change—that is, are the women more contemporary than the men? Specific problems related to marriage, sex, and child-rearing are dealt with in separate chapters.

80

THE MEN VIEW THE WOMEN

Suspicion, Distrust, and Fear of Women

It is difficult, if not impossible, to talk with the men at The Oasis about the opposite sex without feeling that they view women with suspicion and distrust. In many ways these blue-collar men feel the same way about women as they do about Negroes.

One man said: "The trouble with American women is they don't know their place. I was in Japan after World War II and by God those women know who is boss. You tell one of them babes to jump and all they ask is, 'how high?' But an American woman will say, 'why?' "

Another man said: "You take that woman who wants to run the school board.* Hell, when I moved to this town twenty years ago there weren't any women on the school board—it was all men. Now you go up there and the whole damn room is full of women.† No wonder the taxes are going up."

'Women are so damn sneaky," another man said. "You never know what they're up to."

I asked him to give an example.

"Well, you take my wife—if she wants a new sweeper or stove or something like that for the house she won't come right out and say so. Instead, she starts to drag me around the stores until I finally figure out what she's up to—then we either buy the damn thing or we don't. Sometimes it's weeks before I even know what she's looking for."

I asked him if he thought his wife was extravagant in what she bought.

"No, she's a damn good manager, but she's so sneaky. I never know what's coming next."

I asked one of the wives at The Oasis to comment on the above statement. She was caustic: "That woman's husband is so damn tight with a dollar that she'd never get anything for the house if she let

---

*He was referring to a local woman who was a candidate for the school board.

†Actually, as of the 1960s, men still made up a substantial majority of the local school board.

him know what she was up to. Fortunately, he is dumber than an ox and she can usually outsmart him."

You get the feeling that the women, having less power, feel that they have to outmaneuver the men to get what they want.

Some of the men at the tavern seem to resent the position women have won for themselves in American society in recent decades. One man, a plumber, put it this way: "I don't mind their being equal," he said, "but some of them want to run the whole damn show. They're just like the niggers—give them an inch and they'll take a mile."

The men complain that the women are unpredictable and moody.

"I came home the other night and the wife was crying. I figured I must have done something wrong but I couldn't think what it was.

"Anyhow, she was crying so I asked her what the trouble was."

" 'Nothing,' she said.

" 'Then what in the hell are you crying for?,' I asked.

"It took me ten minutes to find out she was crying because she got a letter that her favorite uncle died—Uncle Joe.

"You know how old that old bastard was? Ninety-four! And she's crying because he finally kicked the bucket!"

One man laughed and said: "I'll bet you were scared before you found out what she was crying about."

"Hell, yes, I thought maybe she found out I had ordered that new deer rifle she doesn't think we can afford."

Another man said: "Isn't it funny how women cry over the damndest things?"

Then he added: "The last time I cried was when the Packers lost the championship." The men laughed.

I asked one of the women at The Oasis about this complaint from the men that their wives cry too much.

"Sure, they cry," she said. "If you were married to some of these dumb bastards you would cry too."

She was warming up to the subject.

"These guys don't cry—they get drunk, or chase women, or go shoot a deer or something. But women cry. It's good for them—a hell of a lot better than getting drunk or leaping into bed with somebody."

The men seldom complain that their wives are "dumb": it tends to be the opposite, that the women are crafty, sly, devious, or scheming.

"I never can figure out what in the hell she is up to," one man observed about his wife.

"The other night, for example, I was watching a baseball game on television and I noticed her sitting there in her nightgown brushing her hair—usually she just goes to bed when a game is on but this night she didn't.

"Finally, about the eighth inning, I realized what was up—she was in the mood for some loving.

"I shut that goddam set off in one second flat and in two minutes we were in the sack.

"Now why in the hell didn't she come right out and tell me what she wanted?"

I asked a wife at the tavern to comment on the above incident.

"Well," she said, "women have learned that men like to think of themselves as great seducers. They don't want their wife to chase them all over the house when she wants to go to bed with them, so the women play it coy. They undress in front of their husband, or sit around in their nightgown, as this wife did, and pretty soon the husband gets the message and makes a pass and the wife responds. This makes the guy feel that he is irresistible—which is what they like."

On the positive side the men have certain expressions for a woman they like: she is a "good sport," or a "good mother," or a "good manager," or a "helluva good woman."

One never hears a man at The Oasis make a negative reference to his own mother. He might refer to his father as a "no good sonofabitch" but never his mother. Sisters are usually referred to in a positive tone also. Any hostility the men express toward women is focused either on their wife (or former wife) or on some woman activist in the community.

The Ideal Woman

What sort of woman do these men really want? What kind can they live with happily? Our material would suggest the following ideal:

1. A woman who is content to live along the lines of what some social scientists have called "segregated sex roles"; in other words, in a female world that is largely isolated or blocked off from the world of men.

One man put this point into these words: "I hate a goddamn woman messing in my affairs—always asking 'Where are you going?' 'What time you gonna be back?' I always answer: 'Going where I have to and back soon as I can.'"

2. A woman who is willing to spend time and effort on her home and children. "If there's anything I can't stand," a carpenter said, "it's a woman who keeps a dirty house or lets her kids run loose all day. I figure if a woman can't take care of the house and the kids she shouldn't get married."

3. A woman who keeps herself neat and clean. A wife doesn't have to be beautiful, but she must take some pride in her appearance.

4. A woman who is sexually responsive. Her willingness to have sexual relations when the man feels like it is more important than her appearance or her body. In other words, it is absolute guarantee against sexual frustration that these men are looking for, not beauty or some vague sexual ecstasy.*

5. A woman who is reliable and faithful. When a blue-collar aristocrat spends a lot of time with his male buddies he likes to be sure that his children are being cared for properly and that his wife is home minding her business. Above all she must not be "running around" with some other man. This would expose the husband to ridicule and lower his status in the male peer group.

In general, it would seem that these men like traditional rather than modern women. There is one striking exception, however: almost all (over 90 percent) of these men are willing to have their wives work outside of the home. This represents a modification of the traditional wife model that these men have learned to live with. For some of the older men this change dates back to the economic crisis of the 1930s when they were unable to support their families and their wives had to find some sort of work. For some of the

*See chapter 6 for a more detailed consideration of this.

younger or middle-aged men the acceptance of outside employment by wives and mothers dates back to World War II, when labor shortages and a national crisis made it imperative that wives and mothers hold outside jobs if at all possible.

It could be said that these men have evolved a female model that is extremely functional for them: it allows them great freedom; guarantees them good care of their homes and their children; assures them of sexual satisfaction; protects them against ridicule and gossip; and at the same time gives them economic aid when they need it.

When the writer discussed this wife model with one of the women at The Oasis, her comment was: "Why in the hell woudn't they like a wife like that? It's a damn good deal for them."

One has the feeling that traditional women of the above type are becoming increasingly scarce in American society and that sooner or later the blue-collar aristocrats will have to face the fact that the slaves are in revolt.

Women's Liberation

To say that the drive to liberate women frightens the men in this study is an understatement. As one man said: "It scares the hell out of me." For centuries men have dominated Western society[3] and now they face the prospect that their world, and their power, may have to be shared with women. This prospect leaves them feeling gloomy—or angry.

"What in the hell are they complaining about?" one man asked. "My wife has an automatic washer in the kitchen, a dryer, a dishwasher, a garbage disposal, a car of her own—hell, I even bought her a portable TV so she can watch the goddamn soap operas right in the kitchen. What more can she want?"

Most of the wives at The Oasis are willing to settle for the "good life" described above. They know they have it better than their mothers had it, and the male-female arrangement gives them enough room to maneuver so that they do not feel "hemmed in" or stifled. As one woman said: "If my husband says 'no' to something I can always take him to bed and get a new vote."

One has the impression, however, that the younger women at the tavern are less philosophical about these issues and are more determined to have sexual equality. One of them told me that she claims the same right to "run around" that the men have; she also says that her husband has as much responsibility for their children as she has. This woman is considered a deviant at the tavern now, but sometimes deviants represent the wave of the future.

The older women—those over forty—have very little, if any, tolerance for the militant women's liberationists. This is because the women at the tavern are "gradualists"; they (and their husbands) do not favor social revolution in any form.

One wonders to what extent the attitudes of the men toward women in this study have been formed by the nature of their work: they spend all day, five days a week, in an exclusively male world. I, in contrast, have worked with women (and even under their supervision) for thirty-five years. It could be argued, of course, that being deprived of the company of women all day would make these men anxious to associate with women after work—but this does not seem to be true of the men at The Oasis. These men seem to prefer the company of men.

THE WOMEN VIEW THE MEN

The most common negative reference to the men is that they are "dumb." I once asked one of the women what she meant by this.

"Well, for one thing, they do everything in the book a woman doesn't like and then they can't understand why she loses her enthusiasm for them."

I asked her to be more specific.

"Well, they drink too much; they spend too much time away from home; they often run around with other women; they spend too much money—is that enough or do you want more?"

"Why do you think women marry these men?"

"Because they don't have any choice—the other men aren't any better."

A frequent complaint by the women is that the men drink "too much."

"How often have you seen a woman drunk in here?" one of the wives asked me.

"Four or five times."

"OK. How often have you seen a man drunk in here?"

"Fifty to seventy-five times."

"OK. How would you like to be the little woman at home when daddy comes in with a snootful?"

"Not much."

"OK. That's what women have to put up with.

"And another thing," she added, "if a woman gets too much in here the men think she's *disgusting*—if a man gets too much he's *funny!* I don't get it." She ordered another beer and stared into her glass, contemplating the sad state of the male-female world.

The women complain that the men are "selfish." One woman put it this way: "These guys would go deer hunting if their mother was on her death bed. They think first of themselves. When our kids were small we could never have a birthday party on the right day for one of them because it was the week that the pheasant season opened. Wouldn't you think that kids are more important than pheasants?"

The women also object to what they consider to be sexual promiscuity in the men. This came out when I took a graduate seminar group to the tavern one evening. In the group was a rather vivacious girl in her twenties who made quite a hit with the men. Several of them, married as well as single, danced with the girl, bought her drinks, and plied her with quarters for the juke box.

A few evenings later one of the wives who had witnessed the above incident made a few comments. "That was quite a student you brought over the other night. I thought some of the older men would have a stroke dancing with her. I think Herman* was the only guy that didn't make a play for her."

It is literally true that an attractive woman can excite most of the men at the tavern just by walking in the door. If she is unattached (not married to a regular patron of The Oasis) the atmosphere will be charged with expectation: who will make the approach first? And how?

It may be that attractive men have a similar impact on women at

*Herman is about seventy years old.

the tavern but if so the women conceal their reaction—at least most of them do.

During the years of this study two or three women did appear at the tavern with an obvious sexual interest in the male customers. These women did not conceal their sexual interest, nor attempt to be coy. They were like the men in that their attraction to certain men was highly visible.

The reaction of both sexes to these women was interesting: the men regarded them as "whores" or "sluts," while the wives considered them "sick." Nobody could view them the way similar men are viewed at The Oasis: as people with an insistent sexual need that has not been satisfied.

The basic attitude of men and women at The Oasis toward each other seems to be that of wary distrust. They know they need each other, but at the same time they are never sure how an alliance or truce will work out.

DIFFERENTIAL SOCIAL CHANGE AND THE TWO SEXES

To what extent are the two sexes truly compatible or incompatible? Man's ancestors were mammals and primates, neither of which are noted for close and continuous male-female association. Of course, man's great plasticity makes it possible for him to adapt to almost any cultural system if he has been properly socialized. But at the same time there must be some behavior systems which are more congenial to males than other. As Orville G. Brim, Jr., says, it is easier to make a boy out of a boy than it is to make a boy out of a girl.[4]

Is male-female "togetherness" what men really want or is it something they will have to accept because modern society cannot function under any other arrangement?

It is not being suggested here that males are superior to females, or that sexual equality is not a desirable goal. The question is whether men like to spend their free hours with their own sex or the opposite sex.

It is difficult to talk with the men and women who frequent The Oasis without feeling that somehow these two groups of people are not very compatible. The men in this study prefer the company of other men.[5] They are fiercely independent, determined not to be domesticated or henpecked by a "damn woman," and the women are equally determined not to be relegated to some nineteenth-century Victorian family style that their feminine ancestors struggled to overthrow.

To phrase this in sociological language one might say that these two sexes, at the blue-collar level, have experienced differential social change during the last few decades: the women have had a glimpse of equalitarian marriage as portrayed in the soap operas and in women's magazines and have liked what they have seen, whereas the men have been horrified (or frightened) by the same glimpse.

And so the battle lines are drawn, with each couple carrying on the struggle in their own way. One wife said that she first began to feel like a *person* after her marriage when she took a job and established her own checking account. "I was damn sick and tired of being dependent on my husband for every dime I needed," she said. "When I first got my own checking account, opened with my own money, I used to go around town buying little things for the kids and myself and writing a check for every little purchase—I was like a child with its first allowance. It felt wonderful."

With some couples the struggle for equality leads to bitterness, and the marriage may be terminated. In other cases the wife concedes defeat and retires to her home and her children. And in a few, the man surrenders, knuckles under, and is seen at The Oasis no more.

This struggle, or conflict, can best be seen among the young couples who have begun rearing their families. If the man continues to spend a lot of time at the tavern when his wife is busy with preschool children, it is apparent that he has won the struggle and has emerged victorious, his freedom and independence intact. But if the man seldom appears at the tavern after his first or second child has arrived, then it seems likely that his wife has prevailed. If the young father reduces the amount of time he spends at the tavern, then the chances are that some sort of compromise has been reached.

This battle or struggle is often not apparent in young married couples who have not had their first child; at that point the wife is still employed outside of the home, has her own income, and retains much of the freedom and independence she had while single. The big test for these couples comes when they begin to have children—and one has the impression that some of the marriages begin to slide downhill at this point.

Margaret Mead has argued that no human society has ever really achieved sexual equality.[6] Efforts toward this end have characterized American society since at least the latter part of the nineteenth century, reaching a climax at the end of World War I when women won the right to vote.[7]

In subsequent decades they also won the right to smoke, drink liquor, enjoy sex, go to college, work outside of the home, and divorce their husbands for a variety of reasons. Out of this social revolution has emerged the so-called "modern American woman."

In the past this struggle for emancipation on the part of women has been experienced largely at the middle- and upper-class levels in American society, but now it is also being fought out at the blue-collar level. Thus many of the skilled workers at The Oasis are only now facing demands from their wives that white-collar men had to face decades earlier.

It has been stated many times in this book that these blue-collar aristocrats are extremely independent persons—in the mass society they refuse to be homogenized. Maybe it is because they know, or sense, that the computer will never replace a good bricklayer; that toilets will always have to be installed by a plumber; or that only a skilled carpenter can make your house look the way you want it to.

And yet one has the feeling that eventually these men are going to lose their fight against social change (out of deference to them we will not call it progress). They are opposed to sexual equality, racial equality, mass production of houses, and many other features of modern society. In a very real (or literal) sense these men are *reactionary*—that is, they yearn for the America that began to disappear yesterday or the day before. One can see this in their attitude toward women, in their gloomy view of the welfare state, and in their hostility toward blacks demanding equality. Perhaps this generation of blue-collar aristocrats can survive free and undomesticated in their marriages, but their sons may be in for a rude awakening a few years hence.

One thing seems clear: the parents of these men did not prepare them to live happily with modern women, to enjoy them as companions (except in bed), while the women were not properly socialized to be good companions for men (even in bed). One is reminded of a point made by David Riesman and his associates in *The Lonely Crowd*:[8] namely, that some parents socialize their children for a world that no longer exists. This would seem to be what happened to some of these men. It may turn out, as our society changes, that the two sexes will become completely compatible, even at the blue-collar level. But this does not appear to be the case today.

6 The Sexual Way of Life

"Almost any sex is better than no sex at all."
Statement by a male customer at The Oasis

ʃ

INTRODUCTION

In this chapter an attempt will be made to delineate the basic sexual norms held by the men and women who frequent The Oasis. Some of this material was noted briefly in earlier chapters but the bulk of the sexual material has been reserved for this chapter.

Obviously, it is easier for a male researcher to talk with men about their sex life than it is to talk with women—and this was especially true at The Oasis since most of the female patrons were the wives of the male customers. Much of the material on male behavior was obtained when no women were present (Saturday mornings, for example), when the men felt free to say exactly what they wanted to about their sexual experience. In contrast, the sexual information from women was obtained largely from discussions (or arguments) when both sexes were present. The writer readily admits the limitations of the sexual material pertaining to women at The Oasis. The male data, however, seem to be relatively authentic.

In the original Kinsey studies of sexual behavior in the United States, conducted in the 1940s, considerable emphasis was placed on social class variation.[1] In the present study almost all of the informants represent the same socio-economic level in American society—the stable blue-collar elite. Where possible, comparisons will be made from our limited data to the findings of the Kinsey research group.

It is difficult in this study to assess changes over time in the sexual norms of the men and women at The Oasis because the bulk of the persons represent only one generation, that of the World War II era. In the concluding chapter of the book a few observations on changing sexual norms will be presented, based on the younger persons who began to frequent the tavern toward the end of the study.

WHYTE'S SLUM SEX CODE

In the 1940s William Foote Whyte published what he called "A Slum Sex Code."[2] His observations were based on young Italian men of a low socio-economic level. It seems useful to compare the sex code of our sample with that of Whyte's "corner boys," even though the two groups occupy quite different positions in the social class structure.

There were six cardinal features of the male sex code of Whyte's lower class men:

1. Men marry virgins.
2. Girls need to be protected, and men have an obligation to protect them if they are "nice" girls.
3. There are two kinds of women, "nice" girls and "bad" girls. The "bad" girls are subdivided into three subtypes: "One-man" girls, promiscuous girls, and prostitutes.
4. Men lose status and self-esteem if they patronize a prostitute.
5. Men gain status if they "make" a woman from a higher social class.
6. Men have to have regular sexual satisfaction if they are to remain healthy.

THE BASIC SEX CODE OF THE BLUE-COLLAR ARISTOCRATS

Virginity Is a State of Affairs to Be Ended As Soon As Possible

The writer has never heard chastity defended *for either sex* at The Oasis, except for children. And even then, "if a girl is big enough, she's old enough, and if she's old enough, then she's big enough."

A man at The Oasis once described in considerable detail how he began his sex life at thirteen having intercourse with a young married woman. This account met with approval (if not envy) from the other men present. A white-collar man who was at the bar on this occasion said that he had not "had a woman" until he was nineteen. The blue-collar men present were surprised at the late date. In the Kinsey research of the 1940s and 1950s it was concluded that boys from blue-collar background tend to begin their heterosexual activities earlier than boys from middle-class families.[3] This seems to be true for the men at The Oasis. My data indicate that the average man at The Oasis had his first heterosexual affair by the age of sixteen, with a range from thirteen to eighteen years. In this group a boy who has not "had a woman" by the end of high school is considered to be retarded in his sexual development.

There are humorous "defloration" stories told in this group which describe how a certain boy "lost his cherry." "We fixed Joe up with this widow who was putting out around town and she taught him the facts of life. When he came back from the date he was white as a sheet. He had to buy all the beer that night!"

It is considered unhealthy for a boy to be eighteen or over without some heterosexual outlet. "Something" might happen to him. It is never very clear what this "something" refers to, but it appears to have reference to the possibility of homosexuality.

If a girl is a virgin, a man should try to seduce her.* "If you don't, some other guy will—and then you'll be sorry you didn't."

Implicit in this attitude is a belief that no woman in our society can remain a virgin very long once she starts going out with men. And since her virginity is sure to be taken by some man sooner or later, it might as well be you.

If a boy is a virgin he should try to remedy the situation as soon as possible. By no means should he get married without previous sexual experience; this might make it difficult for him to know how to "satisfy" his wife.

Men Do Not Marry Virgins

I have never heard a man at The Oasis argue that a girl should be a virgin when she gets married. In fact it is difficult to imagine any of

---

*They, of course, exclude young children from this discussion.

these men dating a girl seriously for any length of time who was unwilling to have sexual relations—this would reflect on the man's virility. It would also put the girl in a dominant power position that she might try to perpetuate after the marriage.

Another problem about marrying a virgin is that she might not be very passionate: a girl who can retain her virginity once she is "in love" with a boy is probably not "very hot."

Whyte's corner boys said they would not marry a girl who was not a virgin. There are a number of factors which might explain the different attitude of the men in this study: Whyte's research was done over thirty years ago, and sexual norms in the United States have changed significantly since then; Whyte's men were Italian in ethnic background and female virginity has always had a special fascination for Italians;[4] Whyte's men were all Roman Catholic whereas the men in the present study are of mixed religious background; and, finally, the blue-collar aristocrats in this study occupy a much higher position in the socio-economic system than did Whyte's corner boys.

A Girl Should Not Be a Virgin but at the Same Time She Should Not Be Promiscuous

Like Whyte's corner boys, blue-collar aristocrats divide women into two types: good (or nice) women and "bad" (promiscuous) women. But the "nice" girls need not be virgins; they merely have to choose their sexual partner (or partners) with some care.

The "bad" women are sexually promiscuous; they sleep with almost any man who propositions them. As a rule these women are to be avoided because (a) no status in the male peer group is achieved by "making" them, and (b) they are not capable of being loyal to a man—they will "cheat" on you. And a man loses status in this group if his woman goes to bed with somebody else.

Another difference between Whyte's men and the men in this study is this: the blue-collar aristocrats do not really differentiate between "sluts" (bad women) and prostitutes—to them, a promiscuous woman is a "whore," whether she charges for her sexual favors or not. To some extent this attitude reflects the thin line that currently exists in our society between the promiscuous amateur woman and the prostitute; both are using their sexual favors to get what they need out of men and are viewed in that context.

Sex Has Very Little (If Anything) to Do with Love

The expression "making love" is not used by the men at The Oasis when referring to sexual intercourse. They have a colorful assortment of terms which do refer to this behavior but none of them include the word "love." One can only conclude that for these men sex is sex: it refers to a physical (or organic) experience between a man and a woman. If affection accompanies the sexual act, this is a bonus, but the main ingredient is passion (sexual desire).

To these men, sex is a physical need, and sexual satisfaction refers to physical relief, not psychological fulfillment.

A Normal Man Needs Sexual Relief to Remain Healthy

Except for elderly men, this principle is taken for granted. Any man in the prime years of life who disputed this point would open himself to the charge of being "abnormal."

A Double Standard of Sexual Morality Is Assumed to Be the Normal State of Affairs

This principle is related to the above; a man *has* to have regular sex to remain healthy, whereas this is not necessary for women. This means that a man is justified in taking sex where he can find it if his wife (or his girl friend) is not providing sexual relief.

This belief in the sexual needs of men versus those of women leads to a justification of adultery on the part of husbands while this right is denied wives. In other words, a woman who seeks extramarital sexual partners is a "slut," whereas a man who engages in the same behavior is "starved" for sexual relief by his wife.

It is recognized that some husbands are sexually inadequate, and the wives of such men may be justified in seeking other sexual partners. But this is regarded as unusual, not common.

Prostitution Is a Necessary Evil

A man is not honored for going to a prostitute; this means that he was unable to seduce an "amateur." As one man put it: "I sure as hell will never pay a woman to go to bed—hell, I think they should pay *me!*"

It is recognized, however, that a man in the armed forces, or under some other unusual circumstances, might have to resort to prostitutes, but this carries no prestige in the group.*

It follows from the above that most of these men believe in legalized prostitution; they think it meets the sexual needs of a certain category of men in our society.

Masturbation Is Also a Necessary Evil

It is better, of course, if a man "can find a woman" (almost any woman) to satisfy his sexual needs, but if this is impossible, then masturbation is "better than no sex at all" (as one man put it).

There Is No Justification for Homosexuality

The writer has heard almost every type of sexual behavior defended at The Oasis except homosexuality. Adultery, prostitution, and even incest are accepted within limits, but nobody speaks a word in behalf of the homosexual—male or female. This strikes one as remarkable in a group that seems to be "emancipated" in its attitudes toward human sexuality.†

Married Women Are a Special Prize in Seduction

In this group special satisfaction is obtained by the seduction of a married woman. Since there is always some hazard in adultery, only

---

*A truck driver at the tavern once admitted that he had sought sexual relief from a prostitute while on the road. The men accepted this but felt sorry for the man because he could not find a woman who wanted to go to bed with him.

†This attitude toward homosexuality is discussed at greater length later in this chapter.

the more daring members of the group pursue this sport. If they are not caught, their achievement (if known to others) carries prestige in the group.

It also seems to be true, as Whyte found, that the seduction of a married woman of a higher social class carries special satisfaction and special recognition. One could develop a point system for scoring seductions in this male subculture. The scale would look something like this:

Type of seduction	Points
Married women	
Higher social class	15
Same social class	10
Lower social class	0
Divorced or widowed women	0
Single women	
Virgin	15
Nonvirgin	5

The Cardinal Rule in Sex Is Not to Be Stupid

While it is recognized that sex is a wonderful way of life, it is also recognized that sex (as well as liquor) can ruin your life. Thus a married man whose wife catches him having an affair is not immoral—he is "stupid."

A man who gets a girl pregnant that he does not intend to marry is also "stupid." "The dumb bastard," one man said of this predicament, "didn't he ever hear of rubbers? A man's pecker can get him into a helluva mess if he isn't careful."

The most "stupid" man of all, however, is a man who marries a promiscuous woman and then doesn't realize she is "running around" with other men. In one famous situation of this nature at The Oasis the following comments were heard: "What in the hell did he think would happen when he took that job out of town? Did he expect her to screw herself? You know damn well that babe will get her screwing somewhere."

Another man made the following observation: "That dumb bastard hardly got out of town before she was down here sitting at the bar—all dressed up. I hear she hits a different tavern every night."

Some Types of Rape Are To Be Defended

These men have an ambivalent attitude toward rape. While they do not approve of males using force to obtain sexual favors from a female, at the same time they believe that many forcible rape charges are fictitious—that the woman "had it coming to her."

"By God," one man said, "if I were on a jury the woman would have to prove her case. A lot of women lead a man on until he can't control himself and then they yell *rape*. Bullshit, I say."

Another man said: "Did you ever try to screw a woman that didn't want to screw? It ain't easy, I can tell you. They can put up a hell of a fight. Take my word for it.

"Of course," he added, "if a man uses a knife or gun that's a different story. Then the sonofabitch deserves a good stretch in the state prison."

One man remarked, humorously, that he had been raped several times by women. "I can't help myself," he said. "When they threaten to make me walk home or beat me up I just give in. You might say that I rape very easy."

The men at The Oasis are also skeptical about statutory rape. Many of them feel that the age of consent for girls is too high—eighteen in this particular state.

"Jesus Christ!" one man said. "I picked up a broad in Denver once when I was in the air force and later on I found out she was only fifteen. She was in an adult bar when I met her—how in the hell was I to know she wasn't old enough to screw?"

"They should tatoo their birth date right on the girl's belly at birth," a plumber said. "Then a man would know whether they're old enough or not."

"Why don't they issue the girls ID cards like they do for bars?" another man said. "The card could say 'I am old enough to screw' or 'Don't screw me—I'm not old enough.' "

"That's a good idea," the bartender said, "but some guys in here don't read too good, especially when they're loaded."

"You could make the cards different colors," the other man said.

"Red for the young ones and green for the old ones."

"Some guys are color blind," the bartender pointed out.

Kinsey claimed that statutory rape was a common experience for the American male. It is easy to believe listening to these men.[5]

The men do not, of course, approve of adults who molest children sexually; their argument is that some girls (and boys) mature sexually at a very early age, and they feel that the courts should take this into account in statutory rape cases.

DIVORCED MEN AND WOMEN

The men and women at The Oasis take it for granted that divorced or widowed persons "going steady" are having sex relations.[6] This causes no comment at the tavern. In fact, comment would result if such a couple were *not* having an affair. A divorced man said: "If I had three dates with a divorced woman and couldn't go to bed with her I'd feel impotent."

The basic attitude seems to be that divorced adults of both sexes need sexual relations and are entitled to them whether remarried or not. It would seem that fornication statutes, which prohibit heterosexual relations between unmarried adults, have no support in this group.

Camping trips and vacation trips by divorced couples who are not married produce no comment at The Oasis. It is assumed that such persons are testing their compatibility for marriage.

Divorced or widowed persons at The Oasis may also live together without comment if their behavior otherwise is "respectable"—that is, if they are employed, do not drink excessively, take care of their children (if any), and are not promiscuous in their sexual relations.

As Morton Hunt has demonstrated, the world of the divorced adult is a strange new world; the norms for single youth do not apply, nor do those of married couples.[7] A moral code is, however, apparent for such couples at The Oasis. It is flexible but it exists.

THE WOMEN LOOK AT SEX

One evening at The Oasis a man of fifty or so announced that he was going home to watch television, "after which I intend to make a pass at my wife." All the men present seemed to think this was the way to spend "a perfect evening" (as one man put it), but a married woman at the bar took exception. She had had a few drinks and her tongue was a bit loose. "You guys are nuts," she said to the man who had announced his plans for the evening. "All you think about is sex. Here you are, fifty years old, and you talk about going home and making a pass at your wife. Christ, you ought to be over that by now."

Most of the men at the bar groaned at this point. One man became belligerent. "That's the trouble with you goddamn women!" he shouted. "Soon as a man gets to be forty or fifty you want to shut it off, to make a damn priest out of him. No wonder the guys run around looking for a piece all the time. You women make me sick."

It was clear that most (if not all) of the men present supported the male customer in this argument. The other women at the bar maintained silence.

In the years of this study three or four "promiscuous" women have been observed at the tavern—women who are known to be sexually available to almost any male who might make advances to them. These women are not regular patrons of The Oasis; they show up from time to time with some man who is usually not a regular customer of the tavern either.

As pointed out earlier in the chapter, the men at The Oasis have no respect for these promiscuous women. Neither do the women. The regular women patrons can't imagine how the average man could even touch such a woman, to say nothing of going to bed with her.

In contrast, most of the men at The Oasis are potentially promiscuous sexually in that they would seldom refuse a sexual opportunity that is not too repulsive or too dangerous. They certainly do not view with disfavor men who are sexually promiscuous—in fact they tend to admire such a man if his taste in sexual partners is good and if he doesn't get into any trouble.

"You know that ____ who comes in here?" one man said. I nodded.

"Well that son-of-a-gun gets more tail than all the rest of us put together in here. Good looking women, too. I don't see how he does it."

Notice that the speaker here doesn't ask *why* the other man is sexually promiscuous; he wonders *how* the man can manage it. In contrast, a woman who is sexually promiscuous may be thought of as being "sick"; they wonder *why* she engages in such behavior.

The promiscuous man referred to above is popular with the other men at The Oasis. The reason they admire him is that he has been able to sustain a good marriage with an attractive wife while engaging in numerous extramarital affairs. If such a man "got into trouble" by his sexual activity the other men would no longer admire him. By "trouble" they mean that (1) his wife divorced him, or (2) some man caught him out with the man's wife, or (3) he lost his job as the result of some sexual escapade.

In contrast, it appears that the married women at The Oasis do not admire women who "cheat" on their husbands—unless the husband "had it coming to him." This means that the man was neglecting his wife and/or going out with other women, so "he got what he deserved."

Why do the men at The Oasis seem to be obsessed with sex? One hypothesis would be that high sexual interest carries prestige for men in tavern society; it is a bad thing to be uninterested in sex or "over the hill" sexually. Another hypothesis would be that taverns (and bars in general) tend to attract men who are highly motivated sexually. A third hypothesis would be that American men in general are frustrated sexually and that this frustration is readily apparent in a tavern study.[8]

It seems that the basic difference between male and female attitudes toward sex at The Oasis results from the differential priority assigned sex: the younger men rank it first, and "way ahead of whatever is in second place," while the younger women place sex among the top three or four items in their life. For the women, children, a good marriage, and a nice home are just as important as a good sex life.

Whatever the factors may be that produce the differences, it seems that the men and women at The Oasis have substantial disagreements over the part that sex should play in human society.

A LIBERATED WOMAN

Promiscuous women who come into The Oasis are ostracized by the regular female customers. In 1970, when the women's liberation movement was making headlines, a young woman of twenty-seven or so began to frequent the tavern. In a conversation with me she revealed that she was divorced and that her child was being reared by her parents.

"I should never have gotten married," she said. "I was pregnant and wanted to have an abortion but my parents talked me out of it. They kept yelling at me about motherhood being sacred and all of that bullshit." She paused to light a cigarette and order another beer.

"I started screwing in high school and just loved it—I still do. Not just one man but different men. My husband was good in bed but it got to be monotonous sleeping with the same guy every night."

"Are you attracted by men's bodies the way men are to women's bodies?"

"Yes, I am. When a guy walks in that door I look him over. Some of them appeal to me and some of them don't but I don't know why. One guy I'm sleeping with now is fifty years old and homely as hell but he does something to me. I don't know what it is."

"You sound like the men in here."

"Sure I do. I'm always wondering how some guy sitting at the bar would be in bed. Do you think I'm terrible?"

"Well, I don't think the local PTA will ever honor you as Mother of the Year."

"You can say that again."

This young woman insisted that she had the same sexual rights as men. She also felt that fathers had as much responsibility as mothers for young children. After a few exciting months this liberated woman disappeared from The Oasis. One had the impression that both the husbands and wives were relieved—they felt safer now.

CONVERSATIONS ABOUT SEX

Sex is a favorite topic of conversation among these men (perhaps all men in our society). I would estimate the four most commonly discussed subjects to be jobs, people, sports, and sex—not necessarily in that order. The men tell a great many "bar stories" with either an implicit or explicit sexual content: "Did you hear the one about the new young parish priest and the nun? Well, it seems . . . "

These men "kid" each other about alleged sexual prowess or impotence—"he can't cut the mustard any more." An older man made this remark when he left the bar to urinate: "Well, I'll go back and shake hands with the unemployed." Since he was heading for the men's room I didn't get the significance of this statement for a minute or so; it was, of course, a reference to sexual inactivity.

There is quite a bit of "joshing" among these men about their sexual ability: the younger men tend to brag while the older men often comment on their declining sexual capacity. Sometimes the older men will reminisce about how great their sexual capacity was in their younger days. I have never heard any man in the tavern admit that he was sexually inadequate as a *young* man; this sort of remark can only be made by or about older men, sixty or over.

References to the size of the penis are not rare, in particular the implication that some member of the group is better endowed than others, or that somebody has an unusually small penis. In the latter case the usual reply is: "It's not what God gave you but what you can do with it that counts."

These men often tell humorous stories about their sexual ineptitude when they were young and inexperienced—for example, how "dumb" they were in not having taken advantage of some earlier sexual opportunity. These stories always carry the same point: the teller is not that "stupid" any more.

These workers are mostly veterans of the armed forces, and they talk a great deal about their sexual experiences while in military service: World War II, Korea, the Japanese and German occupation periods. Most of these anecdotes imply that foreign women are easier "to make" than are American women. One has the impression that every living American veteran had at least one exciting sexual affair while in the armed forces.

Stories about how a man lost his virginity are common at the tavern. Quite often it appears that the young man was more or less "seduced" by an older woman. Here is the story of the man mentioned above who was seduced in his early teens:

"I was 13 years old when I got my first piece of ass. I was plowing a field in the hot sun and the dust was flying all over hell. There was a young married couple living in a house next to this field and as I came down by the fence on the tractor this woman waved for me to stop. She wanted to know if I was thirsty and said she had some lemonade in the kitchen.

"Well, I was thirsty as hell and over that fence I went.

"When we got into the kitchen she kept talking about her husband working out of town and how lonely it was living out in the country.

"When she brought the lemonade over to me she sort of brushed herself against me and that did it—my peter jumped right up and before I knew what happened we were in the bedroom.

"After that I screwed her every night until her husband came back to town. Then they moved away and I never saw her again."

Stories like this seem to cast a magic spell over the men as each one recalls his youth and how he lost his virginity.

Stories about passionate women are popular: women who bite, or scratch, or moan, or cry while having sexual intercourse, or women whose sexual desires are insatiable. "This gal I had out in Frisco during the war was really something. We would knock off a piece when we went to bed—and by God about twenty minutes later she would start fooling around to see if I was ready to go again.

"She would wake me up two or three times a night to see if I was ready. Christ, I had to go back to the base to get some sleep."

Then he added: "Sure as hell wish she lived around here."

At this the other men laughed:

"Like hell you do," one man said. "A woman like that would put you in the grave inside of two weeks!"

The original speaker just smiled.

"What a way to go," he said.

A great many stories with sexual themes are told at The Oasis. The following is typical except that it is "cleaner" than some of the others.

"Do you know why prostitutes are now putting zip codes on their stomachs?"

"No."

"Because it makes the male come faster."

End of joke.

ADULTERY AND THE TAVERN

One would expect a certain amount of extramarital sexual activity in a tavern, and the acute observer will not be disappointed.[9] Some of the operations are so skillful, however, that a casual observer would miss the byplay completely. Here is an example.

One Saturday morning an older man appeared in The Oasis with a woman much younger than himself, and a woman who literally exuded sex appeal. The man was very well dressed and made a distinguished appearance. He gave one the impression of an affluent man on his way down. Although sober at this time of day (about 11 A.M.) the man seemed to be more or less an "alcoholic"—if the term includes people who drink too much for their own good.

The woman was provocatively dressed in form-fitting slacks and a tight sweater. She immediately began playing dance music on the jukebox, much to the annoyance of the regular customers nursing a hangover from Friday night (she had broken the unwritten rule at The Oasis that the jukebox should not be played before noon on Saturday out of deference to the heavy drinkers who are suffering from the night before). Being the end of the work week, Friday night calls for serious drinking, and the jukebox doesn't help the next morning.

If a regular patron had started to play the jukebox this Saturday morning there would have been sharp repercussions, but since the man and woman were essentially strangers (the bartender told me later that they had been in once or twice before), nothing was said.

The woman wanted to dance but her male companion said he didn't feel like it.

I glanced around the bar to see who would make the first move towards this attractive woman.[10] The answer was obvious: a young, attractive carpenter who was rather notorious for his sexual exploits was already in action. His first move was to ask the woman to help him pick out some good selections on the jukebox—this is a gambit often used by men trying to make contact with a woman in the tavern. While they were alone at the jukebox they could be seen talking together.

When they left the jukebox the woman asked her male companion if he minded her dancing with the younger man and received permission. After a few dances the woman and the younger man began to play shuffleboard together. The older man moved from the bar to a table near the shuffleboard and continued drinking.

I kept wondering how the young carpenter would "set up" a

future contact with the woman since the older man was only a few feet away. Here is how he did it: When the shuffleboard game was over the three persons sat down together at the bar. The woman began to talk about carpenter work that needed to be done "at our house," at which point the young carpenter offered to come over "some day next week" to estimate the job. He then wrote down the name and telephone number of the man and the woman. Having accomplished his objective, he bought them both a drink and visited with them socially until they left the tavern.

There are two observations that need to be made about this little romantic episode: (1) the woman involved was "unattached"—that is, she did not belong to any of the regular habitues of The Oasis, and (2) her male companion was not physically strong enough to drive off the sexual aggressor; he was an older man who would have been no match in a fight with the younger man.

There is a sort of "pecking order" in these taverns that determines what man may approach what woman. A strong man, known to be a good fighter, need not fear that the other men will approach "his woman"—at least not at the tavern in his presence. They may meet secretly somewhere, but not openly.

A man who cannot defend "his woman," however, will be forced to watch while the stronger and tougher men approach her openly while he is present.

If a man is known to be "dangerous"—that is, might use a knife or a gun—then his female companion will not be approached, even though she may flirt openly with other men in the tavern.[11]

Earlier in this chapter it was reported that some of the blue-collar aristocrats take particular pride in being able to be intimate with a married woman or a woman who "belongs" to another man. It is not only the sexual enjoyment that they covet; it also testifies to their position in the "pecking order" of the tavern society.

HOMOSEXUALITY

One is impressed by the violent attitudes of the men at The Oasis toward male homosexuals. The following conversation is typical: "We had this fairy in our outfit when I was in the Navy. One night at a bar in San Diego we got drunk together and the sonofabitch reached over and put his hand on my cock. I knocked that bastard off his bar stool and half way across the room. The sonofabitch never bothered me again."

Another man at the bar said: "Those bastards better stay away from me. I'd rather fight than switch."

The worst thing you can call a man at The Oasis is a "queer" or a "fairy." A man has to fight or leave the tavern if somebody calls him a homosexual.

It appears that a blue-collar male of this group cannot merely refuse a homosexual advance; he has to physically punish the person making the offer. This reaction does not seem to be very common among middle-class males.[12] How does one account for this behavior complex at the elite blue-collar level?

According to Freudian theory violence toward the homosexual betrays fear on the part of the violent person: Freud postulated that all humans have deep homosexual drives and that strong personal and cultural barriers are required to repress these drives.[13]

I once tried this Freudian theory about homosexuality on one of the amateur sexologists at The Oasis with rather dramatic results.

"What crazy bastard said that?" he asked.

I replied that the great Sigmund Freud had propounded this idea as long ago as 1900.

"The guy was probably a queer," the man said. "No normal man would say a thing like that."

If one accepts the Freudian hypothesis concerning this violence toward homosexuals how are we to account for what seems to be a sharp difference between elite blue-collar male and white-collar male reactions to homosexual advances? One possible explanation is that physical violence in general is tolerated (and even expected) in the blue-collar male world, whereas it is relatively taboo in the male white-collar world. For example: I have witnessed many violent fights at The Oasis during the five-year peiod of this study, but in some thirty years of observation in middle-class bars I have never seen a physical brawl between two male customers. It may well be that middle-class men feel just as hostile toward homosexuals but express their feeling in different ways—by slander and office gossip, for example.

Actually, there are other ways of viewing this hostility toward homosexuals among these blue-collar men; certain kinds of behavior, such as homosexuality and communism, seem to be beyond their realm of comprehension. We have heard threats of violence toward "commies" at The Oasis—is this to be interpreted as fear of Communist tendencies within themselves?

The "Goosing Complex"

There is what might be termed a "goosing complex" at The Oasis that I have never observed in middle-class bars. One man will sneak up on another man and "goose" him in the anus with reactions that are almost hysterical or violent. Usually the episode will end with the men laughing but sometimes a fight is narrowly avoided. Some men are much more sensitive to "goosing" than other men: one truck driver would almost cry if "goosed" more than once in a short span of time.

How is this behavior to be interpreted? Does it represent repressed homosexuality as some psychiatrists would argue? Or does it simply represent the physical "horseplay" so evident in this group—brief wrestling matches at the bar and tests of strength of all kinds? I do not know the answer to this question.

Attitudes toward Female Homosexuals

Female homosexuals are seldom referred to at The Oasis. The men imply that they regard the leaders of the women's liberation movement as lesbians, but this expresses primarily their hostility toward equality for women rather than any knowledge or experience with female homosexuals.

The women at the tavern impress one as being more tolerant of female homosexuals than the men are of male homosexuals: the female customers regard lesbians as being "sick," not threatening.

7 Children and Kinfolk

"The main thing is not to spoil kids."
Statement by a father at The Oasis

CHILD REARING

Various social scientists have concluded that child rearing systems in the United States vary from one social class level to another.[1] In general, these studies have concluded that blue-collar parents tend to be "traditional" in their child rearing philosophy, emphasizing such traits as obedience in their children, whereas middle-class parents are reported to be more "modern," stressing qualities such as "growth" and the uniqueness of each child.

In his classic analysis of American society, *The Lonely Crowd*,[2] David Riesman developed a useful typology of parental models: those who reared their children to be "inner directed" versus those who reared their offspring to be "other directed." The first of these systems seems to be equivalent to "traditional"—be at peace with your conscience—whereas the second might be labeled "modern"— be at peace with your peers. To put it another way, the one system stresses "salvation" while the other emphasizes "social adjustment."

In one of the more elaborate contemporary studies of parents, Daniel Miller and Guy Swanson conclude that modest income parents rear their children to fit into large bureaucratic organizations that tend to dominate American society whereas more affluent parents try to rear their children to understand social systems and operate effectively within them.[3] And in his analysis of social class and family life, Donald G. McKinley takes a critical stance toward

110

some of the studies which have reported significant differences in child rearing between the different social classes in our society.[4]

It can be hypothesized that a trend toward a mass society has produced a homogenization process that is obliterating social class differences in America, including those related to child rearing. Some of this chapter will be devoted to an examination of that hypothesis.

MEN OUT OF BOYS

Fathers and Sons

In other chapters of this book it has been argued that the men at The Oasis reflect an earlier style of life that is tending to disappear in our society. If this is true, how do they socialize their male children, toward the past or toward the future? It is my thesis that most of these fathers are trying to preserve their way of life by teaching their boys the same code the men have lived by. This code has the following features:

1. *Defend yourself physically.* Among these men, physical strength and "guts" are primary male attributes. Any boy who grows up to be a "sissy" is a failure.

"My boy came home from school the other day with a cut lip," a mechanic said. "I asked him what happened and he said this other kid hit him. I told him that if he didn't go back and lick that other kid the next day I would whip him when he got home."

"What happened?"

"He licked the other kid and nobody has bothered him at school since."

"Did your wife approve of how you handled the situation?"

"Hell, no, she wanted to report the cut lip to the school principal. I told her she could raise the girls but to leave the boys to me."

This is a typical attitude among the blue-collar fathers at The Oasis: to become a "man" a boy has to learn to fight, to defend himself, and to give back at least as much punishment as he takes. If a boy doesn't learn this, he will be weak and tend to be "victimized" all his life, not only by men, but also by women.

2. *How to handle women.* As these men see it, one of the great

hazards a boy faces in this world is the chance that "some woman will take him for a ride." In other words, she "will make a fool of him." The woman might trap the boy into a forced marriage,* or even worse, she might "henpeck" him after marriage. One way to protect yourself against women as you grow up is to seduce them. This idea stems from the belief that a woman who can resist a man sexually is in a good position to dominate him.

These men share the belief of the British upper class that boys should never be reared by their mothers or other women,[5] since they will make a "goddamn sissy" out of him. Since these men do not have the English boarding school system to rear their sons, they have to improvise. In the past, one of their strategies was to get the boy out of school as early as possible and get him on the job with other men, but this has become increasingly difficult as the craft unions have begun to require a high school diploma for entering apprentice programs.

If you can't get the boy out of the school system and away from the "goddamn women teachers," then the next best bet is to get him into school athletics, especially football. One man, a sheet metal worker, put it this way: "I'll say one thing for that football coach up at the high school—he makes those guys get down in the mud and go at each other. By God, that's what they need to get along in this world."

Some of the mothers at The Oasis are afraid their sons will "get hurt" playing football, but the fathers see the risk just the other way: the boy will be damaged if he doesn't participate in sports and learn how "to be a man."

3. *Don't be a sucker.* These men see American society as a tricky world and boys have to learn to be "on guard" at all times. They have to learn how to identify a "phony" and how to distinguish an honest crap game from a crooked one.

Actually, the skill and knowledge required to shoot craps or play poker represents a fairly accurate model of what these fathers try to teach their sons: life is one big poker game and to win you must (a) know your own hand—its weakness, its strength, and its possi-

---

*Actually, they tend to believe that all marriages represent a "woman's trap." See chapters 3-5.

bilities; (b) estimate your opponents with some degree of accuracy; (c) know the odds for any given hand; (d) have the courage to play the hand as you see it.

4. *Above all, don't spoil a boy.* Life is too rough for any kid who has been catered to or "spoiled" by his parents, especially boys. Children have to learn early that the outside world is a rough place, and the sooner they learn this the better. This tends to be a "sore point" between these men and their wives. "My goddamn wife is trying to spoil our kids," a plumber said. "If a drop of rain falls, she rushes up to the school to give the kids a ride home. I told her kids *like* to walk in the rain, but she's afraid they'll get a cold or something."

Mothers and Sons

Many of the wives who visit The Oasis do not agree with their husbands on rearing boys. This disagreement has three sources:

1. The mothers are more middle-class in their life style than are the fathers: they read middle-class magazine articles on rearing children, and some of them watch television "soap operas" that are exclusively upper middle class in content. All of this means that these mothers tend to reflect such ideas as "the unique worth of each child."[6]

2. Another source of stress between these fathers and mothers over rearing boys is that the mothers visualize their sons primarily in the roles of husband and father—in other words, the mothers are socializing their sons for family roles. The fathers, in contrast, see their job as preparing the boy for the outside world—occupational role, military role, and so on.

3. The last source of stress on rearing boys derives from the fact that these mothers do not fully accept their husbands as ideal male models for their sons; the wives feel that their husbands do not devote enough time to their families, which means that the mothers are trying to rear sons who will be different from their fathers. In contrast, the fathers like their way of life and are struggling to preserve it for their sons.

There is no easy way to mediate this conflict. Each couple works it out as best they can.

WOMEN OUT OF GIRLS

Fathers and Daughters

Most of the men at The Oasis are content to leave the rearing of their daughters to their wives. It would seem that these men prefer sons to daughters and that their primary concern as a parent is that their sons "be brought up right."

These men do, however, have a few ideas about rearing girls, which might be summarized as follows:

1. Girls don't need as much education as boys. Most of what a girl needs to know can be learned at home from her mother. This means that any money spent on college should go to the sons if possible. This attitude poses certain problems:

a. The daughters tend to make significantly higher grades in high school and are more likely to be accepted for college.*

b. The mothers tend to be more oriented toward middle-class goals, including college for their daughters.

c. The fathers do not provide a good role model for daughters who might be capable of going to college because, for the most part, the fathers are "anti-intellectual"—that is, they value "practical" knowledge over "book learning."

2. Girls, as well as boys, should not be "spoiled." This means, essentially, that they should learn to respect and obey their parents, and they should not be "catered to."

"The other evening I caught my wife doing the dishes while our teenage daughter was sprawled in the living room watching TV. I told her to get the hell out in the kitchen and help her mother with the dishes. I don't want any fifteen-year-old *queen* in my house."

3. Girls should learn not to trust men, especially where sex is concerned. These men feel that they know men too well to trust any of them with their daughters.

---

*This observation was confirmed by the local high school guidance department.

It is my impression that these men have little expectation that their daughters will remain virgins until married; their hope is that she will not become involved sexually with "some bum." Actually, they believe that a "nice" girl's first affair often leads to marriage, and this makes it extremely important that she choose her first sex partner with care. Essentially, this is the same approach they take with their sons: "don't be a damn fool and let some character take advantage of you."

Mothers and Daughers

The mothers want their daughters to be "nice girls." This means, basically, that the girls should find a "good husband" and become a "good mother." Thus most of the emphasis in rearing girls is on preparation for family roles—those of wife and mother.

These mothers are practical enough to know that a woman today will have to earn money at some point in her life, hence it is well for her to acquire some skill: typing, hair styling, bookkeeping, nursing, etc.*

A girl has to learn how to "handle men." Men tend to be difficult and the better girls understand them the better off they will be. The mothers tend to be oriented toward the white-collar world, and it is my impression that they favor white-collar marriages for their daughters.

GENERAL OBSERVATIONS ABOUT CHILD REARING AS VIEWED BY THE MEN

1. These blue-collar fathers have none of the "martyr complex" found frequently among middle-class parents—the idea that "I would do anything for my children."[7] This was quite evident when a $200,000 swimming pool was being considered as part of the addition to the local high school. A majority of the blue-collar men opposed the project. As one of them put it: "We swam in the lake when we were kids and by God they're no better than we were." In sharp contrast, almost all of the middle-class organizations in the

*Note that all of these are white-collar (or white-blouse) occupations. In contrast, the sons are often encouraged by the fathers to learn a blue-collar trade.

community supported the pool project. The bond issue was defeated.

2. These men emphasize obedience in their children. They want their offspring to be "nice kids," although a boy is expected to "sow a few wild oats" when he is old enough to go out with girls. A carpenter said: "I wouldn't give a damn for a boy who didn't raise a little hell when he was young. If he doesn't get it out of his system then, he may do it later—and that will play hell with his wife and kids."

3. There is very little respect in these men for "experts" on child rearing. This includes school psychologists and psychiatrists—the latter are usually referred to as "head shrinkers" at The Oasis.

4. These men do not subscribe to any psychiatric or child psychology mystique about rearing children. They believe that love and firm discipline should produce a "good kid." If this doesn't work there is something wrong with the child, not the parent. One man, a plumber, expressed this view: "They're always talking at school about whether we understand our kids. By God, I think it's more important that kids understand their parents."

5. These fathers exhibit relatively little guilt or anxiety about their parental role.[8] In part this reflects their reliance on tradition in rearing their children: tradition has stood the test of time. If it worked for their parents, then it should work for them.

6. These men do not want their man-wife relationship sacrificed to the parent-child relationship. In other words, if there is a conflict between the woman's role as wife and her role as mother, these men would like to come first. Elliot Liebow found this to be true of low-income black men also.[9]

7. These men rear their children to be "inner directed" (to borrow Riesman's phrase), to pursue their own way of life regardless of what other people think. This reflects the fiercely independent stance of the fathers. Among other things children have the right to remain in the blue-collar world if they want to. One man said: "If my boy wants to wear a goddamn necktie all his life and bow and scrape to some boss, that's his right, but by God he should also have the right to earn an honest living with his hands if that is what he likes."

This "inner directed" approach to child rearing is quite different from the "bureaucratic adjustment" system reported by Miller and Swanson for middle-class parents in Detroit.[10]

DYSFUNCTIONS IN THIS CHILD REARING SYSTEM

There are obvious problems in this parental model, as there are in other parental models in our society. One problem results from the fact that blue-collar jobs are not increasing as rapidly as white-collar jobs in the American economy; in fact, in some segments of industry blue-collar jobs are actually decreasing.[11] This probably means that not all of the sons of these men can be apprenticed to the various trades. If not, will their fathers be able to help them maneuver into a good slot in the white-collar world?

Another dysfunction in this parental model is that some of these children exhibit capacities for growth and learning that are never developed; the goals set for them are too easily attained. This, of course, may simply reveal the writer's middle-class bias, but several of the blue-collar fathers themselves have expressed this point. "I know my kid is bright," one man said, "but we don't push him very hard and he'll probably end up a plumber like his old man—but I guess he could do a lot worse."

These fathers might be criticized for preparing their children for a world that is disappearing, but most American parents would be found guilty on the same grounds.

It is my belief that the mothers in this group are more realistic in their parental role, they are oriented toward the middle-class values that appear to be increasingly dominant in American society. It seems clear that a constant source of stress between these fathers and mothers is their divergent approaches to preparing their children for the adult world.

Orville G. Brim, Jr., has criticized parent education programs in the United States for being almost exclusively middle-class in their orientation; they have assumed that all parents subscribe to white-collar norms regardless of the parent's position in the social class system.[12] The data from this study would certainly support Brim's position that all parents in American society do not subscribe to the same values in rearing their children.

One of the reasons why the fathers at The Oasis express hostility toward school counselors and social workers is their belief that these people employ only middle-class values in their contacts with blue-collar children and their parents.

Even if one recognized that the blue-collar world is shrinking in our society, the fact remains that it still exists and will continue to do so indefinitely. It would be helpful if some white-collar professionals would remember this.

GRANDPARENTS

Among the blue-collar patrons of The Oasis, the role of grandparent seems to be by far the most satisfying relationship in family life.[13] In talking with almost any of the older couples, the subject of grandchildren will usually come up.

"Did you say you taught at the university?" a woman said to me. "My granddaughter goes there—she's in the School of Nursing. Here, let me show you her picture—maybe she'll turn up in one of your classes some day."

The photograph showed an attractive young woman of nineteen or twenty. The grandmother smiled as I commented on the picture.

Why is the role of grandparent so satisfying? One reason is that grandparents can *spoil* their grandchildren; since they only see them occasionally, the grandparents can cater to the children and play the role of "the good guy." Parents, who have to live with the child day in and day out, are forced to discipline their children, thus playing the role of "the bad guy."

One young mother at The Oasis put this into these words: "When the children come home from a visit with their grandparents, I have to fight with them for a day or two to restore law and order. I hate to do it but you can't live with them otherwise."

Another reason why the grandparent role is so satisfying is that young children, as a rule, are cute and full of promise for the future—which means that the grandparents can always hope that the world of tomorrow will be better than the one they have experienced.

Many of these grandparents (like the rest of us) have suffered disappointment and/or tragedy either in their own life or that of their children, and this leads them to focus (or project) their hopes on their grandchildren.

There is one nice feature about this view of grandchildren: most of the grandparents will not be around when the final results are in, and they can therefore keep their dream unshattered. This feature is not true of the biological parent role today; most of us now live long enough to witness how children "turn out."

Not all grandparents are as fortunate as the ones discussed above. Here is the other side of the coin:

"My one son got killed in the war and his wife ran off and deserted the children. The welfare offered to put the kids in foster homes but my wife and I wouldn't hear of it. So the judge appointed us guardians and the children came to live with us.

"It's pretty hard on people our age taking care of three little kids," he continued, "but we sure as hell weren't going to turn them over to strangers."

"Do the children ever hear from their mother?" I asked.

"Not a word. They have never had a birthday card or a Christmas card—not a damn word."

This man finds it hard to understand how a mother can walk out on her children. It makes him wonder about the "younger generation."

KINSHIP

Family ties (relationships based on blood) are quite strong and enduring among the blue-collar workers who frequent The Oasis. My hypothesis would be that these bonds are more meaningful at this level than they are among white-collar middle-class people.[14]

This can be seen most strikingly on holidays such as Decoration Day when the tavern is almost empty.

"Where did you go for the holiday?" somebody will ask a friend.

"Oh, we went over to Black Earth for the day—one of my sisters lives there and she was having a big dinner for my dad—it was his birthday."

At Thanksgiving, various patrons will announce that they are going "up north"* or "back home" for the holiday, or else some of their relatives "are coming down for the day."

---

*Over a period of several decades economic opportunities in the state have been shifting to the southern areas, which accounts for so many of the customers coming from "up north."

One has the impression that the kin network is still highly functional for these people; it meets some of their needs to belong, and it helps protect them against the anonymity of the mass society.

"Are you related to the Zieglers up by Lodi?" somebody will ask.

"Christ, yes, all those people up there are my relatives—cousins, aunts, uncles—the whole works.

"My grandfather Ziegler had fifteen kids and those hills are full of Zieglers—all of them related. When we have a family reunion up there you never saw so damn many Krauts in your life."

One reason why kin relations loom large in the lives of these people is the size of some of their families.

"We had 11 kids in our family," a truck driver said, "and all of them are still living. Hell, I got brothers and sisters living all over this part of Wisconsin. I could drive from here to Superior and never have to buy a meal or pay a motel bill—and get drunk every night without buying a drink."

After a pause he added: "Maybe I should take that trip this summer—those guys are always coming down here and drinking my liquor."

This man's wife's family had seven children, so between the two there are eighteen sets of uncles, aunts, brothers, sisters, brother-in-laws, and sister-in-laws.

Two Brothers

An illustration of the strong kinship ties among this group may be seen in the following case. Two brothers who frequent The Oasis have worked together for fifteen years as carpenters, plasterers, masons, and carpet installers.*

The older brother told this story:

"When my mother died she made me promise to take care of my little brother. Since that time he and I have worked all over the world together—Hong Kong, Reno, Miami—you name it and we have worked there. I promised my mother I would take care of that little bastard and that's what I've done."

---

*They hold union cards in all of these craft unions.

The younger brother (who was about thirty-five) nodded his head and smiled. Then he said: "Tell him about some of the times when you got drunk and I had to take care of you."

The older brother laughed. "That's true, by God," he said. "A Mexican in Texas might have killed me if my brother hadn't got me out of a crap game before all hell broke loose."

These brothers own a camper truck and use that for temporary living quarters when they move from one job to another.

"If you ever get to Vegas," the older brother said, "and stay in the Stardust or any of them big hotels—my brother and I put most of that wall-to-wall carpet in. In the summer, when it would get up to 120 degrees, we got up at 3 A.M. and worked till noon—but that was on concrete blocks, not carpet."

I asked the brothers why they had come back to their home state. The older one replied. "I wanted to see my kids," he said. "Their mother and I have been divorced for twenty years and I haven't been around much since then."

Then he smiled and added: "One of my daughters is married now and had a baby boy and I just had to come home to see what that little stinker looked like."

The two brothers came into The Oasis for several months (the proprietor had known them years before) and then disappeared once more for other parts of the world.

Factors Which Support Kinship Relations in This Group

The following factors seem to enhance kin relationships among the blue-collar workers at The Oasis:

1. *Rural and farm background.* It has been pointed out elsewhere that a majority of these men and women grew up on farms or in small rural villages. This means that as children they were literally surrounded by relatives and tended to internalize this way of life.

2. *Large families.* The families of birth seem to have been relatively large for this group, and this in itself tended to emphasize lateral and vertical kinship ties.

3. *Social class continuity.* Most of these men and their wives grew up in either farm homes or "working-class" homes, which

means that they have not migrated to a different social world: they did move to the city and did enter the urban occupational structure, but they work with their hands and their bodies just as their fathers and grandfathers did. In short, they are still members of the "working class"—and proud of it. This means that they have much in common with their relatives, most of who remain at this same social class level.[15]

4. *Geographical stability.* When Americans move up in the social class system they tend to move *away*, thus separating themselves spatially from most of their relatives. They may still have affectional ties for their kinship group but a distance barrier tends to limit their interaction.

For the most part, this barrier does not exist for the customers at The Oasis—modern highways and fast automobiles make it easy for them to visit back and forth.

5. *Weak association ties.* Various studies have revealed that blue-collar people are not "joiners" to the extent that middle-classers are.[16] The data on this group confirm this finding: these people belong to a church, a trade union, and perhaps a fraternal order (such as The Moose) or a conservation club. They attend the fewest meetings possible and try to avoid "entanglements." In some ways their kinship relations tend to replace association memberships.

ETHNIC BONDS

Ethnic background is a constant factor at The Oasis—you feel its presence almost every day.[17] A majority of the regular customers are either German or Scandinavian. Most of the ethnic comments are intended to be humerous—unless you are Polish, in which case they are not very funny.

"Oh, he's a dumb Swede," somebody will remark. "You have to make allowances for them guys—they don't know much."

This remark would normally be made by a German and would bring an instant response:

"All the dumb Swedes are still back in the old country—the smart ones like us came over here."

"Jesus Christ! If the smart ones came over here, I'd sure as hell hate to see the rest of them."

This sort of bantering may go on for ten or fifteen minutes.

The conversation will usually end with somebody telling a "Polish joke." The Poles were one of the last immigrant groups to enter the state and are located primarily in industrial areas such as Milwaukee. They are seldom seen at The Oasis and are the butt of most of the ethnic jokes.

"Did you hear about the two Poles who got fired out of Oscar Meyer?* Seems like they were in charge of boiling the pigs feet and lost the recipe."

"Do you know where to insert the hose if you want to give the world an enema?"

"POLAND!" is the automatic response.

Once in a while the Poles strike back. There is a story about a man who stopped at a tavern in South Milwaukee † to have a bottle of beer. As he looked around the tavern he was amazed to see what looked like a stuffed man in a cage in one corner of the tavern.

After having a few more beers the customer finally asked the bartender:

"Say, what in the hell is that stuffed man in that cage over there?"

"Oh, that," the bartender replied casually, "that is the last customer who told a Polish joke in here."

There are very few (if any) Jews who frequent The Oasis and they are also the target of hostile ethnic stories. Anybody who is close with money at the tavern may be referred to as "my Jewish friend."

The Germans in this area are somewhat unusual in that most of them are Roman Catholics who left Germany after the Protestant Reformation.

If blacks are regarded as an ethnic group in our society they would rank below Poles at The Oasis.

This constant reference to ethnic background at The Oasis impresses me because one hardly ever hears ethnic background mentioned in informal conversation at the university where I am employed. It seems that beneath the "humor" of the ethnic comments at The Oasis is a belief that some behavior in our society has to be understood within an ethnic setting. A painter, for example, said

---

*A large meat packing plant where some of the customers of the tavern work.

† Largely Polish.

this: "You take those goddamn Norwegians down by Stoughton—
they won't hire a damn German like me to paint their house. Your
name has to be Olsen or Anderson to bid on them jobs."

It is interesting to note that this ethnic flavor at The Oasis persists
in spite of the fact that most of the customers' families arrived in
America several generations ago.

8 Tavern Social Life

"You only go around once in this world."

Statement by a customer at The Oasis

INTRODUCTION

The men at The Oasis—and some of the wives—are determined to have a good time in this world, partially because they have so little faith in the next one. As one of them often remarks: "You only get one throw of the dice in the game of life and you better make it a good one." Most of these men are convinced that the world is going to hell and they are trying to salvage what enjoyment they can from "one hell of a mess."

In the terms of Herbert J. Gans, these men like to be "where the action is":[1] they want to enjoy today and let tomorrow take care of itself. This stance toward life can be seen in the men when they are nursing a "hangover"; they may be suffering severely, but they usually stress what a good time they had the night before. And they don't vow "never to do that again"; they just say that "next time I'll be more careful."

One of the sources of stress in the marriages at The Oasis results from the fact that the wives have a somewhat different view of life: They tend to put duty and honor before enjoyment, whereas the men reverse these priorities.

It is my belief that one source of the hostility these men have toward the white-collar middle class results from the middle-class code of respectability and responsibility: the effort to straighten out

125

the world in terms of middle-class values. These men tend to think that the world should be enjoyed, not reformed.

One man expressed this posture toward life in talking about sex. "Honey, I said to my wife, this is too big for us to understand, let's just relax and enjoy it."

In this chapter the focus is on the social life that centers in and about the tavern. The reader will see that it is very rich and constitutes a major life activity for those who participate in it.

BOWLING

During the period of this study the owner of The Oasis sponsored two bowling teams—one for the men and one for the women—which competed in local leagues. The teams would often meet at the tavern for a drink before going to the bowling league. They usually returned to The Oasis for a few beers after bowling. If a team had a good score that particular night the first round of drinks would be "on the house." At the end of the bowling season each team had a bowling banquet financed from a "kitty" built up during the bowling season.

The women's bowling team usually competed in a state tournament at the end of the regular season. The men were more likely to enter tournaments in the local area.

For the team members, bowling provided a lot of amusement. Other tavern regulars would sometimes go to the bowling establishment to root for the team, and bowling scores were often an item of conversation at the tavern. "You should have seen old Mel knocking over the pins last night. He had just enough beer in him to see a little crooked and that did the trick. He couldn't miss."

SHUFFLEBOARD

Shuffleboard is a nice game for couples to play: the men may play as partners against the women, or the couples will split up, so that a wife shoots against her husband with the other man as partner. The games are usually played for a small wager, the losers having to buy a drink. They also have to put the money in the machine for the next game.

Some of the shuffleboard players at The Oasis are quite skillful and at one time (before this study) one of the tavern regulars competed in a national shuffleboard tournament. Some of the better male shuffleboard players like to play for a dollar a game, and I have seem a few games played for five dollars a game. The owner frowns on such large bets but they occur nevertheless.

POOL OR POCKET BILLIARDS

There seems to be a perpetual pool game in progress at The Oasis. In fact, this was one of the original attractions of the tavern for me. A game called "eight ball" is invariably the choice of the players. During the period of this study the owner sponsored a pool team in a metropolitan league, and one year the team won the league championship. When matches are played some of the regulars from the tavern will come and root for their team, even when the match is away from home. With only a few exceptions the wives do not shoot pool; it is almost exclusively a male activity at The Oasis.

I played on the pool team for three seasons and soon learned that the secret of winning matches was to stay relatively sober. Play begins at 8 P.M. and the matches often last until 11:30 or so, which means that a considerable amount of alcohol can be consumed before the shooting is over. Very often the team that wins is simply less intoxicated during the last few games.

It is an interesting fact that a person's pool game, as observed at The Oasis, reflects his personal and social adjustment of the moment. One man, an excellent pool player, lost consistently during a period of unemployment; another skilled player began losing to almost everybody when his wife sued him for divorce; a third man's game deteriorated rapidly when he became ill and the doctors could not diagnose his illness. He was dead within a few weeks of stomach cancer and gave up pool entirely once he learned the nature of his illness.

In William Foote Whyte's study of street corner boys (really young men) he discovered that a person's status in the group reflected his ability to compete in games such as bowling.[2] This is certainly true of the men (but not the women) at The Oasis. A man does not necessarily have to be a good pool player to enjoy high status in the group, but he has to excel *at something*. This might be card playing, or hunting, or even drinking, but he has to show above average ability in some activity to receive deference in the group. One exception would be physical strength; a powerful man in this society automatically enjoys high status unless he becomes an alcoholic or ruins his life in some fashion.

Women seem to achieve high status in this group by physical attractiveness and their ability to catch (and hold) a high status man.

If you observe the pool players at the tavern closely and over a period of time, you will discover that their style of play reflects their stance toward life. "Big Joe," for example, plays a cautious game. Before each shot, he surveys the entire table to examine the various possibilities, and before shooting he calculates the defense possibilities of each potential shot—what opportunities the opposition will have if he misses his shot. This style also represents Big Joe's approach to life: he tries to avoid being vulnerable, and, above all, he tries hard never to be "a sucker" (his words).

Another player, Handsome Jack, will step up to the pool table, take a quick look at the situation, and bang away. Once in a while he wins, but usually he does not.

The reckless players, when they lose, often use the expression: "That's the story of my life." This is said in a half-humorous, half-serious way; it is *literally* the story of their life in many cases.

CARD PLAYING

There is usually a card game in progress at The Oasis. In earlier days one night a week was set aside for a euchre tournament for married couples but this era was about over when this study began.

Cribbage, euchre, and sheepshead are popular card games. Wagers are always involved. Nobody seems to play cards just for the enjoyment of the game.

One of the most violent arguments I witnessed at the tavern involved a card game in which one of the players was accused of cheating. It is very dangerous to accuse anybody of cheating at The Oasis, a fight usually results.

BOATING

Several of the men at the tavern own a pontoon boat in partnership. The boat is stored during the winter in the lot at the rear of the tavern and a great deal of beer is consumed while the men prepare to either put the boat in the water early in the summer or get it out of the water before the nearby lake freezes over.

"Mel," Bart will say, "this week we *have* to get that damn boat in the water. My wife is raising hell about it—she wants to use the boat for a birthday party for one of the kids."

"Hell," Mel will reply, "we would have got the damn boat in last Saturday if you hadn't started drinking boiler-makers.* I can't put the damn thing in myself."

The men will then begin to reminisce about the good times they have had on the pontoon boat. It is claimed that one year the boat didn't get into the lake until the Fourth of July; and some stories report that one year it had to be chopped out of the lake ice sometime in December.

Most of the men at The Oasis own power boats, and boating (with fishing) is a major activity during the summer months.

HORSESHOES

There is a place in the lot at the rear of The Oasis for pitching horseshoes. Some of the men like to take a six pack of beer and determine, periodically, who is the champion horseshoe pitcher. As usual, bets are placed on the outcome.

GAMBLING

The desire to gamble is very insistent in the men at The Oasis.[3] They will place a wager on almost any event that does not have a certain ending: football games, baseball games, horse races, pool games, shuffleboard, even the outcome of courtship.†

When special sporting events are held, such as the Super Bowl in professional football, relatively large sums of money are bet. In 1969, for example, when the New York Jets defeated the Baltimore Colts for the world championship, several hundred dollars changed hands at The Oasis. An automobile mechanic won $150 on this event, and several other customers won or lost $50-$75.

---

*A "boiler-maker" is a glass of beer accompanied by a shot of liquor.

†I once heard two men bet five dollars as to whether or not a certain couple would ever marry.

A familiar pattern is to form a "pool" on a weekly event such as a professional football game. Each person puts one dollar into the pot and draws a number—one through zero. If a football games ends 14-14 the winning number is 8 (adding the last digits in each number). The holder of the winning number gets all of the money.

This type of tavern gambling is tolerated by the liquor commission in Wisconsin because there is no "take" for the house: if the bartender or the proprietor wants into the pool he has to put his money in as the customers do. If the tavern made a profit from any gambling at the tavern the owner would run the risk of losing his liquor license or having it suspended. This would be disastrous (or at least very costly) economically.

During the period of this study there was no "organized" gambling at The Oasis; that is, no baseball or football or basketball pools on which tickets were sold by an underground gambling syndicate. In an earlier period such tickets had been sold by one of the customers but he had been arrested and discontinued the activity.

For some families the husband's gambling must be a financial liability. I once saw an unemployed truck driver lose $46 of his $60 weekly unemployment compensation shooting pool (eight ball) with a hustler who had strayed into The Oasis and found a "pigeon."[4]

There are men who come into the tavern who seem to be superior card players and/or pool players who apparently visit several taverns weekly for the sole purpose of gambling. I have talked at length with one such person, a pool player, who mentioned several taverns in the area that he visits that frequently. He claims that in a good week he may clear as much as $100 shooting pool. This is in addition to what he earns at his regular job. Once in a while this man loses money shooting pool: "usually when I drink too much and get bombed out of my mind," he says. He claims that he has shot pool for bets as high as $300 a game.

This man was involved in the incident in which an unemployed truck driver lost $46 of his weekly unemployment check of $60. I was present on this occasion and witnessed the process of tavern hustling.

The two men started out shooting eight ball for one dollar a game. The truck driver won two out of five games and lost the other three by narrow margins. He then suggested they play three games for five dollars a game. The hustler agreed. The next three games were close but the hustler won all three. The truck driver then proposed that they play for ten dollars a game. This was agreed and very quickly the hustler won three games in a row. At this point the truck driver was very upset and almost started a fight. He eventually left the tavern and the hustler departed also.*

In order to operate the above hustling game a man has to move from one tavern to another and even from one part of the country to another. This particular hustler has worked in California on two different occasions and in various parts of Wisconsin.

It is obvious that gambling has not been stopped at The Oasis by the passage of antigambling laws, but it is also clear that commercialized (or syndicate) gambling has been kept out of the picture. There are no slot machines or punch boards at The Oasis, no sports pool tickets from the outside are sold, and the owner derives no income from the informal betting that takes place.

It would seem that, given the desire to gamble that is so obvious in these men, the state has been effective in limiting the amount and the nature of gambling that does go on in this tavern. †

Why is the desire to gamble so persistent in these men? What functions does it perform in their lives?[5]

One obvious reason why these men gamble is that it increases *the action*. As one crane operator observed: "A little bet on the total score can make even a lousy baseball game interesting." There is also an element of skill in most forms of gambling, and most of us derive enjoyment from exercising a skill. Status in the group is also a factor: a man who wins more than his share is viewed either as a "lucky dog" or a "sharp cookie."[6] Both terms are positive in determining social status in the tavern.

To a considerable extent, it seems to me, gambling for these men is

---

*There was, of course, nothing "crooked" in these pool games. The one man was simply a much better player than the other man. The hustler, however, will often not play as well as he could when the stakes are small, hoping that the stakes will go higher. This happened in this case when the men began playing for only a dollar.

† A wealthy man who often visits the tavern in the morning for a drink once said to me: "Hell, these guys don't gamble. The biggest crap game in the United States is the one I'm in—the stock market."

a defense against boredom.[7] As "action lovers" their primary goal in this world is to avoid a dull life; this can be seen in their frequent references to various life activities (such as marriage) as a "helluva drag."

Actually, these blue-collar aristocrats are similar to other aristocrats in their fight against boredom: they have gone to the top of their social world and need not expend time or energy in "social climbing." This means that most of them have the time (and the money) to indulge themselves in various activities (such as gambling) which enhance their lives.

I do not view gambling at The Oasis as a form of social deviation— nor do the men. They believe that gambling reflects a deep need of the human spirit, that it should be legal, supervised, and taxed by the state. I am inclined to agree with them.

HUNTING AND FISHING

Most of the men at The Oasis love to hunt and fish. When the deer season opens in the fall there is a mass exodus of the customers as the hunters "head north," and the tavern is almost deserted for a week or ten days until the hunters return and begin to spin their yarns as to how "I got my buck," or, in some cases, "how I missed my buck."

To me, the deer season (and the stories after) are the climax of the year at The Oasis. Before the men leave* the air is full of stories about guns—new guns, old guns, and "gun swaps."

"I've had that old sonofabitch since 1932 and she shoots as true today as she ever did. I wouldn't sell that bastard for a hundred dollars."

'This guy down at the shop sold me this Remington for forty bucks—said he couldn't hit anything with it. I took it out to the Gun Club and bore sighted it and she shoots perfect. The dumb bastard never had the sight aligned properly!"

"My father used this gun and never missed a buck and by God so far I haven't missed one with it either."

To portray the year-long cycle of the men at The Oasis we propose

---

*Some industries in this area don't attempt to operate during the deer season, having learned from past years how many men seem to "get sick" that week.

to follow one man through a typical year. This man may hunt and fish more than the average man at the tavern but he is quite representative of the general attitude that prevails toward hunting and fishing at The Oasis.

Bill is a policeman in the nearby metropolitan community. His occupation influences his hunting in two ways: (1) he is expected to be skilled in the use of firearms, and (2) he can accumulate "time off" and get away from the job whenever the various seasons open.

In the spring Bill waits for the opening of the trout season. He has several favorite spots not over an hour's drive from the tavern, and he fishes these streams methodically. If he catches too many trout for immediate consumption they either go into the family freezer or are given to friends and neighbors.

During the summer Bill fishes several lakes in the area, one of them less than a mile from his house. From these lakes he usually takes "pan fish": perch, bluegills, etc.

But Fall is the time of year that Bill loves: rabbits and squirrels, the pheasant season, and then the exciting influx of Canadian geese, the hunter's dream.* In the Fall Bill lives in a sort of fantasy world. You might hear him say something like this: "Took a drive up toward Spring Green yesterday—saw a beautiful male pheasant strutting near the road. When the season opens next week I'm gonna go back up there and we'll see what happens."

You can be sure he has carefully marked the spot and will be back there on opening day.

"Did you get your Canadian geese tag?" I asked him one day.

"You're darn right—I had my check in the mail the first day they were for sale. I wouldn't miss that for anything."

One day he showed us a Canadian goose he had shot. It was, indeed, a beautiful bird. We asked Bill if he had any reluctance or guilt about shooting the goose. "No, I don't," he replied. "The hunting up there is carefully supervised—there are game wardens all over the place. I wouldn't want any part of it if the birds were being massacred or slaughtered, but this is not the case."

---

*Several hundred thousand Canadian geese stop each fall at a hugh marsh about an hour's drive from the tavern. Special permits are sold to hunt Canadian geese, and the entire hunt is rigidly supervised by both state and federal officials.

Deer season is for Bill the climax of the year, as it is for most of the men at The Oasis.* He takes a week off for the deer season and has not failed to bag a buck for the last several years. He always hunts at the same place, with the same group of men.

The annual pilgrimage "up north" never varies. Bill and his hunting companions leave their homes the day before the season opens and arrive at a farm house belonging to a relative of one of the hunters that night. They have a few beers, eat a good meal, and then hold their annual "reunion,"† reliving the hunts of previous years.

Everybody is up early for the opening of the deer season at daybreak. One year Bill got his buck fifteen minutes after the season opened.

"Well," he told me, "it was the damndest thing you ever heard of. Two years ago I saw a buck at this same spot but he took off before I could get a shot at him.

"So this year I said to myself—do you suppose by any chance that sucker might come back there again?

"Anyhow I found that spot again and had just decided to open my thermos bottle and have a cup of coffee when I looked up and there was this big buck staring right at me, not over fifteen yards away.

"I took one quick look through the sight and hit him right between the eyes—he fell over and hardly took one step. It was the damndest thing that's ever happened to me in all the years I've been hunting."

In a hunting party anybody who gets their buck early in the week spends the rest of the week helping his buddies get their buck.††

On opening day 200,000 or more deer hunters will be in the state forests,§ and fatal shooting accidents are not rare. The men at The

---

*A family crisis was precipitated at the tavern when a girl scheduled her wedding during the opening week of deer season. At first the father announced that he would not attend the wedding; later on he relented and was present to give the bride away.

†Some deer hunters live in various parts of the state and only see each other at the annual hunt.

††In some areas of the state in some years does may also be shot, but the men do not talk about shooting a doe. Only a buck is exciting to hunt.

§There is another variety of hunting during the deer season: this is called "dear" hunting: Men who don't go north for the deer season but use the week for some extramarital prowling. Some of these men swear it beats deer hunting any day.

Oasis appreciate the chance they take but they feel the excitement of the hunt is worth it. "Christ sake," one man said, "everything worth doing in this world is dangerous—friend of mine fell off a bar stool and broke his back, but that's not going to stop me from having a drink when I feel like it."

At this point another man said: "Why don't they have seat belts on bar stools like they have in cars? Then your friend wouldn't have been hurt."

After deer season, six to eight weeks of wonderful story-telling may be heard at The Oasis: who got their buck, who didn't, and all the details of how it happened. Sometimes a hunter ran into a bear, or perhaps even shot one, and these stories are always exciting. "I looked up and there was this big black bear looking down at me from the top of this rock. I was debating whether to shoot or get the hell out of there when somebody else shot and the bear took off. We never saw it again."

There are long conversations as to how deer meat should be cooked, whether bear meat is good to eat or not, and who makes the best venison sausage in the area.

When Bill gets home from the hunt he takes his deer to a small butcher shop in a nearby village and has most of the deer meat made into "summer sausage." He once gave me a piece of this, and it was delicious.

Bill carefully preserves the antlers from his bucks and prepares them for mounting: the antlers are sand papered, varnished, and mounted on attractive wooden plaques. Sometimes he has a metal plate prepared with the year of the hunt engraved on it. These plaques are displayed in various rooms of his home.

With the coming of winter Bill's hunting comes to an end for the year, but he does some ice fishing on the nearby lake "when the mood strikes me."

Bill's wife understands his love for the outdoors and would not think of interfering with his hunting and fishing excursions. She regards him as a good husband and realizes that men can have hobbies that are worse than hunting and fishing.

Some people who don't approve of hunting and fishing regard men like Bill as "ruthless killers" or "despoilers of nature." He does not have this image of himself and does not impress one as cruel or inhuman—in fact, he makes just the opposite impression.

Actually, Bill is a conservationist at heart: he believes in strict regulation of hunting and fishing and abides by the rules established. He sincerely wants to preserve the natural environment for future generations to enjoy as he has enjoyed it.

In defense of deer hunting, Bill points out that under modern game management practices the deer herd in Wisconsin was larger in 1965 than it was in 1920. He sees no reason why fish and other wildlife cannot be protected and preserved by the same methods.

It is a serious mistake to think that Bill merely likes to hunt and fish—he *loves* hunting and fishing. He is an outdoors man who earns his living in a police patrol car but has never learned to like city life. He is the farm boy who still loves the land. There must be millions like him in America.

TAVERN HUMOR

There is a great deal of "joshing" at a tavern such as The Oasis: banter or "kidding" that goes on more or less continuously between certain individuals. Some of this exchange has an ethnic flavor: The Wild Irishman, for example, will stick his head in the door and inquire:

"Is it alright if an Irishman joins the dumb Swedes in here for a nip?"

Then somebody will yell at the owner:

"Harry! For God's sake, can't you do something to keep the trash out of here? Even a public tavern should maintain some standards."

The Wild Irishman will laugh, buy a round of drinks, and the joshing will start.

In this type of exchange it is important to have a good reply; otherwise you are being "put down" by your adversary. Here is an example: The Wild Irishman walked into the tavern one Saturday morning with an artificial red poppy pinned on the front of his shirt—poppies that are sold annually by one of the veterans' organizations to raise funds.

Mel leaned over, looked at the poppy intently, and exclaimed:

"1964! You cheap sonofabitch!" (This was 1967.)

The Irishman's expression never changed.

"Mel," he said, "I sure as hell am glad to see that you can read—I was never sure before."

This ended that particular exchange and everybody laughed. Both sides had scored and nobody got hurt.

Notice that The Irishman did not take offense at the word "sonofabitch" used by Mel. Such epithets are acceptable when used by friends or as part of a humorous exchange. If a stranger called The Wild Irishman a "sonofabitch" a fight would be the immediate result.

Certain members of The Oasis are the acknowledged leaders in the planning of "practical jokes" on members of the inner circle. Mel is one of these leaders. There is a story that a few years ago a male customer was drinking beer at The Oasis and loudly lamenting the fact that he had to leave the comfort of the tavern and sow some grass seed around his new house.

Mel suggested that the man have a few more beers with his old buddies and then they would help him seed his new lawn. According to the story, Mel bought several packs of vegetable seeds and these were put on the new lawn along with the grass seed. In a week or two the home owner was amazed to see turnips and other vegetables sprouting in his new lawn. Gradually he became aware that his old buddies had played a trick on him.

One of the most popular characters at The Oasis is a man sometimes called The Dutchman. Although he has lived and worked in the United States for many years The Dutchman retains a wonderful German accent and patrons at the bar love to get him excited; then the accent becomes even more enjoyable.

During the lunch hour one day some of the men at The Oasis tried to persuade The Dutchman that the Germans did not invent sauerkraut (a dish The Dutchman dearly loves). The men—a group of plumbers—claimed that the Irish had developed sauerkraut. I was present this noon and eventually became involved in the exchange. The Dutchman became so excited that he could scarcely talk.

"No, by God!" he yelled, "the goddamn Irish did not invent sauerkraut—the Germans invent that dish!"

The other men then polled the people at the bar, and it was agreed that, indeed, the Irish had been preparing sauerkraut for centuries and, presumably, had developed the dish. Nobody had ever heard about the Germans having invented sauerkraut.

At this point The Dutchman was beside himself; he could not

believe his ears. "Jesus Christ!" he said to me, "you are a professor, tell these dumb bastards who invented sauerkraut."

My reply was that this bit of knowledge was outside my field of specialty but that I had read somewhere that the Irish had learned how to make sauerkraut from the Romans when they invaded Ireland a long time ago.

The Dutchman was dumbfounded.

"The Romans!" he shouted, "those dumb bastards don't know how to make sauerkraut even today! I went to Italy once and no place could you get good sauerkraut! Those wops are spaghetti eaters—that's all they know how to make."

Somebody at the bar suggested that the Germans might have lost the secret of making sauerkraut, just as the secret of making stained glass windows had been lost during the middle ages.

"Bull shit!" The Dutchman snorted. "Once you know how to make sauerkraut you never forget, never!"

For months after this the "joshing" about who developed sauerkraut was revived from time to time.

Many of the humorous anecdotes at The Oasis relate to the eternal male-female struggle: how a husband "tricked" his wife in some fashion. Here is an illustration.

A man who lives near the tavern sometimes had difficulty getting away from the house to join his buddies at the bar. He finally developed a system for the summer months that worked rather well: he would tell his wife he was going out to mow the lawn, fill the power mower with gasoline, start the mower and park it out of his wife's line of vision, with the motor running. He would then hustle over to the tavern (only a block away) for a few beers with his old pals.

The scheme worked for several weeks until a certain thing happened: the mower ran out of gas one Saturday, and when the wife didn't hear the mower she went out into the lawn to investigate. Her husband, of course, was nowhere to be found.

The men at The Oasis still chuckle about this incident, even though it happened several years ago.

Many of the regular customers at the tavern come from rural backgrounds and some of their humor reflects this. One favorite story of this nature tells how an old farmer was driving his tractor up a hill with a manure spreader hitched behind the tractor. A stranger in a big car who could not pass on the hill because of the slow tractor began to blow his horn and shout at the old farmer to pull over. Without looking back or saying a word, the farmer pulled the lever on the manure spreader and threw cow manure all over the big car behind him.*

In stories such as the above, the rural person always triumphs over the urban person.

Many jokes or stories at The Oasis relate to automobiles, reflecting the prominent part that cars play in American life. One of these involves a Volkswagon. It seems that a worker had bought a new Volkswagon † and was bragging at the plant every day about the wonderful gasoline mileage he was getting. His fellow workers decided to sneak a gallon of gasoline into the new Volkswagon every day or so to inflate the gas mileage.

The owner of the car became more and more elated .

"Sixty miles a gallon!" he announced one day. "That's better than they advertise!"

One day the man said that he was taking the new Volkswagon into the dealer for a regular check-up.

At this point the men stopped sneaking the gasoline into the Volkswagon's tank.

In a few days the owner was furious.

"How do you like that!" he says to his co-workers. "I was getting sixty miles to a gallon until I took the car into the dealer for a tune-up, and now I'm only getting forty miles to the gallon. What do you suppose those dumb bastards at the garage did to it?"

The men pretended to be puzzled and urged the owner to take the car back and complain to the dealer.

This story has no formal ending. The dealer and the owner are presumably still confused as to what happened.

Many of the "jokes" at The Oasis have an ethnic and/or racial flavor. Persons of German descent make disparaging remarks about "dumb Swedes" and vice versa. Poles and Negroes are most consis-

---

*This is a favorite rural-urban story. I first heard it in the 1940s while working in Vermont.

† This would be most unusual. Only one blue-collar customer at The Oasis drives a foreign car. Most of the men there distrust foreign cars.

tently the butt of hostile stories, with women running a close third.

It seems clear that status at The Oasis is related to the ability to "dish it out" in the rapid-fire exchange called "joshing": you have to have a quick retort, and preferably one that puts you "one up" on your opponent. People who can't compete in the game lose status.

PARTIES

In a very real sense there is a "party" every weekend at The Oasis. The men drift into the tavern any time after four on Friday to have a few beers before going home. About six or so they go home to change clothes and pick up their wives: Friday night is "couples night."

About seven or eight in the evening small groups leave to have dinner in a restaurant in the area,* after which most of the couples return to The Oasis to drink, dance, play shuffleboard, shoot pool, or just talk.

Wives who may not be seen at the tavern at any other time will usually show up Friday evening. Even the moderate drinkers will often get "high" Friday night, and the less temperate ones end up with a "hangover" Saturday morning. The heightened tempo continues through Saturday and Sunday, with the tavern returning to normal on Monday.

Many special events are celebrated with a party at The Oasis: one wife gave a big "surprise" birthday party for her husband at the tavern; a widower and his new bride had an informal wedding reception at The Oasis; a large party was held for an old customer and his wife when they retired and moved to Indiana; a father gave a party at the tavern when his son returned safely from the war in Vietnam; former neighbors who return to the community for a visit are entertained at the tavern; relatives are brought in for a few drinks and to be introduced to the group; and so on.

St. Patrick's Day usually calls for a "party" at The Oasis. One year two men who are not even Irish continued the St. Patrick's celebration at the tavern for a week.

"It's because we think the Irish are so goddam wonderful," one of the men explained to me.

---

*The Oasis does not serve complete meals, just sandwiches and soup.

New Year's Eve is, of course, the biggest party of the year at The Oasis. Paper hats and noisemakers are usually provided and at 1 A.M. Harry locks the door and permits the regular customers to continue the celebration as long as they wish (there is no local closing hour on New Year's Eve). Transients who try to get in after 1 A.M. are turned away.

I attended some of the parties at The Oasis. One of them was for the elderly couple who were retiring and moving back to their native state. The women had arranged an ample buffet: baked ham, barbecued beef, buns, baked beans, relishes, brownies, and coffee. If a person had not contributed food he was expected to put a dollar into the container provided for that purpose. Customers bought their own drinks. Some of the men had brought their musical instruments (accordion and guitar) and as the evening progressed couples were dancing their way among the tables near the bar. It turned out to be a very nice party.

Another party I attended was the one given by a father in honor of his son, who had returned safely from the war in Vietnam. A huge kettle of spaghetti and meat balls had been prepared by the father and everybody was invited to help themselves at no charge. People bought their own drinks.

The father was elated that his son had survived the war. "God-damn," he said, "I never thought the kid would make it back." He circulated around urging everybody to have another dish of his spaghetti and meat balls. I accepted his invitation.

TRAGEDY

When the family of a regular customer of The Oasis suffers a tragedy, the group responds. Funerals are attended conscientiously, flowers are sent, hospitals are visited, and funds are collected for the family.

One night I stopped in at the tavern and found the people at the bar talking about a man in his forties who had been a regular patron of The Oasis and was reported to be dying of cancer.

One of the men brought a glass jar over and asked me to contribute to a fund for the man's family. "Lee," he said, "put something in this jar. That poor sonofabitch is up there in that hospital tonight dying of cancer and his four little kids are sitting down in that damn house crying."

Another time a popular member of the inner group suffered a disastrous fire, losing his home and almost all of his furniture and personal property. The regular patrons responded to this crisis with help of various kinds.

Another customer was diagnosed as having active tuberculosis and had to be hospitalized for several months. Visits were made to the sanatorium, and handicraft items made by the person while hospitalized were sold at The Oasis.

In a very real sense the inner core of the tavern's patrons functions as a mutual aid society: psychological support is provided in times of crisis; material help is available if needed; children are cared for; cars are loaned; and so on. In our vast, impersonal society such support and aid are highly functional.

TELEVISION

As a rule, most of the customers at The Oasis prefer that the "idiot box" (as some of them call it) be turned off. It is not unusual to hear a regular customer exclaim: "For Christ sake, Harry, turn that damn thing off. I came up here for peace and quiet and that thing is polluting the air."

If Harry happens to be watching the news or some special event he may reply (with tongue in cheek): "I am only trying to improve some of the minds that come in here—and some of them need it." This is usually said with a smile.

If the event is something quite special—such as a state of the nation address by the president—Harry will refuse to turn the television set off.

Political attitudes can be readily observed when a political program is on television at the tavern. During one of the space team recovery programs, for example, it became quite apparent that most of the viewers at The Oasis felt that the space program was costing too much money and had been given too high a priority. One man said: "I'll be a sonofabitch if I can understand why we have to start exploring the moon when we can't straighten things out on this planet. I don't get it."

The big thing on television at The Oasis is, of course, sporting events: football, basketball, baseball, bowling, boxing, horse racing, almost any sporting event of any consequence will cause the television set to be turned on.

Once in a while, almost by accident, a "soap opera" will be on television while the blue-collar workers are eating their lunch. This invariably produces some caustic remarks from the men.

One noon a plumber watched a soap opera scene in which a woman was planning to have a baby by another man because her husband was sterile. Furthermore, the woman made it clear that she was doing this *for* her husband, so he could be a "father."

When the scene on television ended the plumber shook his head in disbelief and said to me: "I'll be a sonofabitch. Now I know where my wife gets some of her crazy ideas—she watches that crap all day long."

As a matter of fact, all of the daytime television serials (the "soap operas") portray upper-middle-class men and women in a white-collar world, which means that the blue-collar wives who watch the programs and take them seriously* are absorbing values and norms that their husbands do not share. This is also true of the mass magazines read by these women.

MUSIC AND DANCING

There is, of course, a juke box at The Oasis. As a rule the men do not play the box unless there are women present—the men prefer the music of their own conversation.

As a matter of fact, it is women who usually start playing music at the tavern, but once it is started the men seem to enjoy it and they put in most of the quarters. Music, of course, makes some people think of dancing, and soon a few couples will be maneuvering around the tables adjacent to the bar.

The juke box is usually not played during the day time except by transient couples who happen to stop in at the tavern. As mentiond previously, there is a tacit agreement among the men *not* to play the

*Some women at The Oasis have told us that they sometimes watch the daytime serials "for a laugh"; they regard them as ridiculous.

juke box on Saturday mornings when many of the men have hang-overs.*

Most of the music is sad—stories of broken love and unfaithfulness. Johnny Cash is a favorite singer.

The only "happy" songs on the juke box are the old-fashioned polkas—"Roll Out the Barrel—We'll Have a Barrel of Fun," and the like. When these are played The Oasis really jumps and people seem to have a good time.

There is no jazz music as such played on the juke box and very little "rock."

The desire to dance seems to be unequally divided among the married couples at the tavern, which means that the wives often have to find dancing partners among the other men at the bar. As a rule this produces no problems but once in a while a husband may take offense at the manner in which some man is dancing with his wife.

For the transient couples who visit The Oasis dancing seems to be a prelude to seduction—and a very nice prelude, indeed.

THE TAVERN IN AMERICAN SOCIETY

It can be seen from the foregoing that numerous group activities are part of the social life of a family tavern such as The Oasis. The fringe members are usually not included in these activities—only the insiders. In a very real sense a tavern of this type becomes the center of social life for the group, in the same way that a country club does for some middle- or upper-class people.

To achieve the type of intimacy found at a public tavern such as The Oasis several conditions seem to be necessary:

1. Long-term continuous operation by an owner who is well liked by the steady customers. Harry owned and personally managed The Oasis for over two decades. Unless Harry was ill, customers could expect to see him almost any time they stopped in at the tavern. Harry entered into the fun with his customers (except that he drank no alcohol while tending bar), and he was regarded as a member of the group by the inner circle of patrons.

*You can usually determine who has a hangover by observing what the men drink; tomato juice mixed with beer is a common antidote.

Harry used to say: "This tavern is my home. I spend most of my time here. Have a good time—but, remember, you are in my house."

2. An occupational and/or social class homogeneity is needed to produce the social cohesion observed at The Oasis. Since most of the customers were skilled construction workers (with a few truck drivers thrown in), these conditions were readily met. Income, occupational hazards, educational level, economic conditions—most of these men and their families shared a large part of their life in common. This, of course, is not entirely true, because some families experienced tragedy that others escaped, but to a considerable degree the customers of The Oasis faced the same world.

3. Stable residential patterns are necessary to create the primary group relationships found at The Oasis. While this particular community was experiencing a mass invasion of white-collar families during the period of this study, the blue-collar residents, for the most part, had lived in the area for twenty to thirty years. As a matter of fact, Harry had often known the parents of some of his younger customers.

Thus, the inner core of customers at The Oasis are not a transient group. I have heard some of them say, "This place is good enough for me. I expect to stay right here until they put me under the ground."

In mass society one of the crucial needs of the individual is to defend himself against the impersonal world around him: to feel that he belongs, that people know who he is, that somebody cares about him.[8] For its regular patrons, at least the inner circle, The Oasis performs this function quite well.

The tavern offers more or less uncritical acceptance of the individual—within broad limits. If your spouse doesn't like you, or your children reject you, a person can usually find a tavern where the customers are friendly. This feature should not be discounted in considering the function of the tavern in modern America.

Another need of the individual in modern society is what to do with his leisure time. This is quite apparent at the tavern in talking with men who spent their childhood on a farm. One man put it this way: "Hell, we didn't have any problem of what to do with our time on the farm—we worked all the time. Now a guy works forty hours a week and has the rest of the time for himself." The Oasis satisfies some of the leisure needs of the men (and women) who congregate there.

One way to view the men at The Oasis is to see them as first-generation city dwellers. In their conversation it is clear that many of them still yearn for the wide open spaces. "When I retire," one carpenter said, "I'm going up north and buy me a piece of land out in the woods and build a cottage and just enjoy the scenery. I've had all the city life I want."

Most of these men literally hate large cities such as Chicago or New York. "I wouldn't live in Chicago if they paid me $50,000 a year," one plumber said. "It wouldn't be worth it."

One of the features these men like about the town The Oasis is located in is that it is an old community, not a brand-new suburb.

In a more religious society the social life of these people might revolve about the church. But modern America is increasingly secular and the tavern is ready-made for such a society.

One dictionary defines a club as "a group of people associated for a common purpose, usually in an organization that meets regularly. The room, building, or facilities used by such a group."[9] Judged by these criteria The Oasis is a club indeed.

9 Drinking Patterns at the Tavern

"In heaven there is no beer—
that's why we drink it here."
Song on jukebox at The Oasis

INTRODUCTION

On the first visit to a tavern such as The Oasis an observer finds it difficult to differentiate one drinker from another. Most of the customers drink considerable quantities of beer, and a few display a taste for whiskey and/or brandy.* Repeated visits to the tavern soon reveal an almost incredible variety of drinking patterns among the regular patrons. An examination of these various drinking styles will be one of the features of this chapter.

In the literature on alcoholism it is apparent that one of the problems in this field is that of defining an "alcoholic."[1] This chapter will explore this matter at some length.

The third focus of this chapter will be on the liquor laws in this particular state and the difficulty of enforcing them in a public tavern such as The Oasis.

VARIETIES OF DRINKING PATTERNS

The Beer Drinkers

There is a polka on the juke box at The Oasis which contains these lines: "In heaven there is no beer—that's why we drink it here." It is certainly true that a lot of beer, both tap and bottle, is consumed at

---

*Very little gin is consumed at The Oasis, but there are some vodka drinkers. The state has the largest per capita consumption of brandy in the United States, and brandy outsells whiskey at The Oasis.

147

The Oasis. In this section the different types of beer drinkers found in a tavern of this nature will be analyzed.

There is considerable variety among the steady beer drinkers at The Oasis. One man, a carpenter, said: "I have been drinking a six-pack of beer every day since I came out of the army in 1946. It doesn't make me fat and I like the damn stuff. I suppose they'll have to put a six-pack in my casket when they bury me if they want to give me a good send-off." This man does not like whiskey or brandy and hardly ever touches any "hard liquor." He gets a little "high" on beer at the tavern occasionally but drinking has never presented any problem to him.

One reason why this man avoids "hard liquor" is that he is afraid of it. "I have seen what that stuff has done to some of the guys who come in here and I want no part of it."

There are other men who frequent The Oasis who might be called "beer alcoholics". These men "get loaded" almost every day and one can see definite damage to their lives: some lose their jobs, some suffer divorce, while others neglect their children.

A third type of beer drinker is the person who really prefers the "hard stuff" but uses beer as a defense mechanism. These men do not even think of beer drinking as *drinking;* they consider themselves "on the wagon" if they are consuming only beer. One man said: "I can handle beer—it is that other stuff that kills me."

A fourth type of beer drinker resembles the preceding except that he doesn't drink beer on weekends or holidays—he switches to whiskey or brandy then. Such a man uses beer to keep himself sober during the week when he has to work. A man of this type has a problem when on vacation or when he is not working; he finds it difficult to stay off the "hard stuff" when he doesn't have to go to work the next day.

The "Hard Liquor" Drinkers

Most of the men at The Oasis who exhibit serious signs of excessive use of alcohol do not limit themselves to beer: they have a weakness for the "hard stuff"—whiskey, brandy, gin, or vodka. Very few cocktails are served to blue-collar men at The Oasis; the liquor is either taken in a shot glass or mixed with water or some other mix.

A very common drink is a "boilermaker," which is a glass of beer "with a shot on the side."

The men seem to recognize the hazard in drinking the "hard stuff." They will say "hit me again" when ordering another shot, but they do not use this expression when calling for another beer.

One of the men, when he takes a shot of hard liquor, will say: "Well, here's how we lost the farm."

The former alcoholics and the nondrinkers at The Oasis are afraid of hard liquor: they confine themselves to beer or soft drinks. If somebody offers to buy them a shot they are apt to say: "God, no, I lost my bout with that stuff a long time ago."

One man said: "I used to drink two quarts of whiskey a day. When my wife left me I got some sense and quit. Now I stick to coke; it never leaves me with a hangover." He continues to visit the tavern because he enjoys the male companionship to be found there.

Very little wine is consumed at The Oasis. In spite of the money spent on advertising by the wine industry in recent decades, very little effect can be observed in this tavern.

It is a myth that people cannot become alcoholics on beer alone, but it does seem to be true that the most severe damage from alcohol usually occurs in the customers who switch from beer to "the hard stuff."

The Weekend Drinker

Some of the blue-collar elite workers hold jobs in which the responsibility is so great that drinking during the week is literally prohibited, either by the employer or the job itself. A long haul truck driver made this statement: "The rig I drive cost $35,000 and last week the stuff I was hauling was worth another $50,000. No employer in his right mind is going to put that out on the road with a rum-head at the wheel. If I have even one beer when I'm driving I can be fired on the spot—and there's nothing the union can do about it."

This man also has to operate on a tight schedule. "The load last week had to be at the unloading dock in St. Louis at 8 a.m. Wednesday—or else. I was there at 7:45."

This man admits that on the weekends, when he is off duty, he likes to get "smashed." As a rule he drinks only beer, but lots of it. "I love beer," he says, "and I get so damn thirsty for it during the week I can hardly stand it. So I drink all I want on the weekends."

Another man, a crane operator, said this: "I love the goddamn hard stuff but I don't dare touch it during the week. When you're lifting heavy steel over the heads of your buddies down below you better not have a hangover. The guy before me tried that and he's unemployed now."

This man has operated heavy cranes costing $85,000 and more. He drinks beer moderately during the week but Friday night he starts on whiskey— the most expensive brand in the tavern. "All of my ancestors are Irish," he says, "and the love for that stuff is in my bones."

The Stabilized Drinkers

The use of alcohol is usually considered to be progressive: people begin by using small amounts and then gradually increase their consumption. This is certainly the pattern for the excessive drinkers at The Oasis, most of whom would rather have no drink at all than just one or two.

But one is also impressed by the stability of some of the drinking patterns. A man of about forty-five stops in at The Oasis every day after work (he never misses unless he is sick or out of town on vacation). He always has two shots of brandy and a glass of beer. The proprietor says that this man has been doing this for the last twenty years.

This man has a responsible blue-collar job with a large firm and has held the same job for at least two decades. Nobody at The Oasis can remember when he ever drank more than two shots of brandy on his daily visit. In fact it has become a sort of joke among the men, and they often offer to buy Harold a drink just to see if he will exceed his daily quota. So far he never has.

The proprietor says he has never known this man to drink "too much." It appears that Harold does not drink at home, or at any other tavern.

Another regular customer is a prodigious drinker of brandy. I have seen him drink eight shots of brandy at one sitting without showing any visible effects. He is a large man (not tall but stocky) who gets a lot of physical exercise on the job, and he has been drinking heavily as long as anybody at The Oasis can remember—at least two decades. This man goes to work six days a week at 5:30 A.M. and often works on holidays as well. He now owns his own business. His wife says she has never known her husband to miss a day's work because of drinking.

This man appears to have a good marriage and is obviously devoted to his children. "I love to drink," he once told me, "but you have to watch it. Some of the guys in here hit it too hard. If you can't go to work the next morning you should stick to lemonade."

Another man, a fabulous character at The Oasis, has evolved a personality pattern that makes it impossible for most people to tell whether he has been drinking or not. He is likely to say or do almost anything even when he is sober and this tends to "cover up" his drinking; you cannot assume that he is "loaded" just because he does something that most people wouldn't do unless they were drunk.

It is the general consensus of the other customers that this man probably drinks more brandy, day after day, than any of the steady drinkers at The Oasis,* and yet he has never become an "alcoholic." His marriage is stable and he has held a good job for the last ten years.

Why is it that some steady drinkers never become "alcoholics" while others do? Scientists, of course, have been trying to answer this question for decades, with only partial success. Little is known about genetic or organic factors that may be involved in the desire for alcohol, but at The Oasis the steady controlled drinkers seem to enjoy life, and they use alcohol to enhance that enjoyment, whereas the uncontrolled drinkers seem to be trying to use alcohol to make their lives worth living. This seems to be the basic difference between the controlled drinkers and the uncontrolled drinkers at The Oasis.

DRINKING AMONG THE WOMEN

Harrison Trice estimates that there are probably about five male alcoholics for every woman who drinks excessively.[2] The proprietor

---

*This man has been heard to say: "Hell, I *spill* more liquor than some of these guys drink." This comment has also been used on some television shows.

of The Oasis believes the above estimate to be inaccurate; he claims that he has seen very few female alcoholics in over two decades behind the bar.

Various writers have pointed out that female alcoholism tends to be more "invisible" than male alcoholism: women are not as free to go out to taverns and bars unescorted or alone, which means that some of the excessive female drinkers confine their drinking to their apartments or their homes.

In terms of visibility, men who drink excessively at The Oasis far outnumber the excessive women drinkers; a reasonable estimate would be fifteen to one. Most of the women who frequent this tavern are the wives of regular customers and they appear to drink moderately. Some of them seem to drink only to keep their husbands company, but a few have obviously developed a fondness for beer or liquor.

There are a few women in their fifties or sixties who seem to get "beered up" quite regularly—three or four times a week. These tend to be women who started coming to The Oasis with their husbands after their children had grown up and left home. Such women are hardly ever seen at the tavern alone; they drink with their husbands or another married couple. Very few of these women drink whiskey or brandy.

There are a few women who frequent the tavern who obviously "have a drinking problem"; that is, they need a daily intake of alcohol to keep going and they would find it very difficult to "go on the wagon." For the most part these are either divorced women or women whose marriages are unhappy. One of these women died during this study while in her early forties. This woman would appear at The Oasis several times a week and drink beer until she could scarcely walk. She was not accepted by the other women at the tavern and was also avoided by most of the men.

Several other women who might be labeled "alcoholics" (depending on how you define the term) made their appearance at The Oasis at various times and disappeared. These were fringe members and not accepted by the regular customers.

One "hidden" female alcoholic used to appear at The Oasis about eleven in the morning on weekdays—a time when few of the regulars would be present. She would drink vodka and orange juice and before leaving would buy two half pints of vodka and conceal them in a very large purse that she carried. She explained one day that her elderly mother, who lived with her, did not approve of drinking: "I have to be very careful," she said, "because my mother would be very upset if she knew I drank." This woman's husband was very devoted to her and her drinking did not appear to have any negative effect on their marriage.

It is interesting to observe the impact of steady and/or excessive drinking on marriage. In the situation discussed above, the husband was a moderate drinker who did not seem to resent his wife's abuse of alcohol. Even though she had a serious drinking problem it is doubtful that her husband ever considered her "an alcoholic."

In some cases a sort of "alcoholic couple" syndrome emerges in which both marital partners seem to drink too much, with relatively little damage to the marriage. In other cases, however, one spouse or the other (usually the husband) drinks too much, resentment is seen in the partner, and the marriage is on shaky ground.

As with so many other things in marriage, it appears to be the partner's reaction that determines the impact of drinking on any given marriage.

STRATEGIES USED BY WIVES TO COPE WITH THEIR HUSBANDS' DRINKING

There appear to be three quite different strategies employed by the wives of the men who patronize The Oasis to cope with the drinking of their husbands. These are as follows:

Drink with Your Husband

Some of the wives have decided that they might as well drink with their husbands; they follow the old rule that "if you can't lick 'em, join 'em." These are usually women whose children are relatively grown up and no longer require close supervision.

It is difficult to assess the wisdom or the effectiveness of this drinking strategy; some of these wives seem to have become "problem drinkers" in the process of keeping their husbands company at the bar. One woman said to me: "I started coming here to keep him out of trouble and now I am as fond of the stuff as he is."

A few of these couples get "pretty well oiled" two or three times a week and appear to have a mutual drinking problem: they both drink too much in the process of trying to keep each other sober. These couples tend to be middle-aged and, having discharged their parental responsibility, seem to have the feeling that they can now drink as much and as often as they like.

Married couples often quarrel and/or fight at The Oasis when one or both of them have "had too much" (the proprietor's phrase). Like most middle-aged married couples they seem to have accumulated a number of unsettled conflicts over the years and these tend to come to the surface under the influence of alcohol. A psychiatrist would say that the conflicts and the related hostility are kept repressed most of the time but are released under the influence of alcohol.

Such couples, when arguing at The Oasis, will often call each other "bastard" and "sonofabitch," but the next day they seem to be back on friendly terms. As a matter of fact the marriages of the couples being discussed here (with one exception) have survived from twenty-five to forty years.

It is not possible to say what would have happened to these couples if the wife had not decided to drink with her husband, but the hazards in couple drinking are fairly obvious.

Avoid the Tavern and Don't Drink Alcohol If You Come in with Your Husband

Less is known about these women because their strategy is to avoid The Oasis, and since they don't drink alcohol when they do visit the tavern they are not apt to talk so readily. These women seem to feel that one steady drinker in a family is enough. Some of them are younger women with children of school age who feel that their place is in the home. They have tried to get their husbands to spend more time at home but, having failed, have assumed more parental responsibility themselves.

Some of these wives have become teetotalers as a defense against their husband's drinking; others drink moderately on special occasions. When this strategy is used a matricentric family tends to emerge, with the husband-father on the fringe. Some of the divorces seem to come out of this group.

Visit the Tavern Occasionally and Drink with Your Husband

These women seem to follow a middle-of-the-road policy: as a rule they are not seen at The Oasis but seem to enjoy their visit when they do come. Such a wife may get "high" at The Oasis a few times a year, dance with her husband and his friends, play shuffleboard or shoot pool, and then not be seen at the tavern for several months. They also tend to be women with school-age children to worry about.

It would appear that any strategy employed by the wife to counter her husband's drinking at a tavern involves certain risks.[3] If she completely avoids the tavern she drives a wedge between herself and her husband's friends, with the possibility that she will only reenforce his behavior. The strategy of drinking with her husband is not very practical for the younger mothers, and it also poses problems for some of the older women, as we have seen.

It is quite possible that the strategy employed by any given wife will depend on (a) her stage in the life cycle, or (b) the quality of her marriage. A young wife-mother may avoid the tavern while her children are still of school age, with the expectation that she will eventually spend more time at the tavern with her husband and their mutual friends. If her marriage is too uncomfortable, however, a wife will avoid the tavern, thus also avoiding her husband, take care of the children at home, with the idea of divorcing the husband when the children are grown up. One does not meet these women at the tavern, but you do meet their divorced husbands in their forties or fifties.

A fourth strategy used by some wives can be observed: bring the children to the tavern and drink with your husband. This is not really approved at The Oasis, either by the proprietor or the regular customers, except for special occasions that might be described as "family days." It is all right to bring a child or a grandchild to The Oasis once in a while, but you should not stay too long or do this too often. Persons who do are viewed with disfavor and soon find another tavern that is more friendly.

THE WHITE-COLLAR DRINKERS AT THE OASIS

Some of the most repulsive excessive drinkers who come into The Oasis are white-collar types who are refugees from the middle-class world. These persons represent fringe members of the tavern's clientele: they are not really accepted by the blue-collar regulars but are merely tolerated. One such person is a state government official who frequents The Oasis at noon, knowing that he is not likely to meet any of his professional colleagues at a blue-collar tavern.

The following case is intended to illustrate the white-collar alcoholic that one sees in a blue-collar tavern.

This man formerly owned a large business in the adjacent metropolitan community. Rumors are that his father built up the business and he destroyed it. In any event, this man became an alcoholic several years ago, and the family business was closed. In the process the man declared bankruptcy, which meant that various persons in the area were unable to collect money owed them.

"Going broke" itself can be understood and accepted at The Oasis but for a bankrupt this man appears to live on a somewhat lavish scale. This has led some of the customers to think that there was "something crooked" about the bankruptcy proceedings in this case. As they put it, "the sonofabitch took the bankruptcy law." Some of the construction workers who frequent The Oasis have lost wages from men who declared bankruptcy, and they have contempt for such persons.

The man being written about here has, indeed, become a contemptible figure; unable to drink in his former middle-class bars, he now haunts working-class taverns in the area. He usually gets drunk, becomes nasty, and ends up being asked to leave.

Men of the above type contribute to the "dim view" that many blue-collar customers of The Oasis have of the middle-class world. They see it as a rat race, with the successful rats being chewed up in the process.

Actually, there are blue-collar alcoholics who are just as repulsive as the white-collar man described above, but these blue-collar "drunks" are not usually seen at The Oasis: they gravitate to skid-row type bars where they do not have to face their former colleagues. And this, of course, is precisely what this white-collar former businessman has done: he is no longer seen at the middle-class bars where he formerly did his drinking.

It is interesting to note that in this process of "moving down" as one becomes an alcoholic, steady drinkers do not see the results of excessive use of alcohol; the alcoholics who formerly drank with them tend to disappear.

A pathetic type of alcoholic upsets everybody at The Oasis by his presence because he is a living reminder of what could happen to all of the steady drinkers. This is one reason why bar and tavern operators hate to see "a drunk" walk through the door. It is as if you might see a lung cancer victim at your favorite cigarette counter.

WHO IS AN ALCOHOLIC?

One of the problems in the study and treatment of persons who have a drinking problem has been the difficulty of defining the term *alcoholic*. In the pages to follow several case studies of persons who "drink too much" will be presented.

"The Guy Is a Bum"

A young worker of thirty-two has just been fired by his third employer within a period of 18 months because he drinks excessively and doesn't show up for work. His foreman told me: "The guy is a bum. He has such a hangover on Monday that he might as well stay home. Last Friday about ten in the morning I sent him into the shop to pick up some stuff we needed and he never came back—he got drunk. That's when I fired him. I don't think he will ever get another job with a contractor around here—the word has gotten around that he's a rummy." It is interesting to note that the foreman in this case is a regular customer of The Oasis and drinks heavily himself, *but after work.*

This young worker spent seven years learning his trade. There is a shortage of skilled men in this field, and he could earn $12,000 to $15,000 a year if he could drink moderately and show up for work. But he is unemployed, his wife has filed for divorce and has charged him with nonsupport, he is living in a motel room, and he has been writing "bad" checks. Unless something can be done, his future looks very bleak—at thirty-two. One can only guess at the impact on his wife and children.

The amazing thing about this case is this: there is a great deal of tolerance of excessive drinking in the construction trades—the foreman of this man drinks heavily and several of his crew who frequent The Oasis are hard drinkers—but these men *show up for work*. That is the dividing line between the alcoholic and the heavy drinker among the customers at The Oasis.

I talked with the young worker one day while shooting a game of pool with him. He was very depressed. "I don't care any more," he said. "Piss on it. My goddamn wife left me with a pack of bills to pay and all I do is work and turn the money over to her lawyer. It's no damn good."

After the game he went back to the bar and proceeded to get "bombed." That same week he cashed a "bad" check at The Oasis and was not welcome there after that. He then disappeared from the tavern: one reason was that his former work buddies came in almost every day and he didn't wish to face them.

This young man should be in a treatment program for alcoholics but he is not. It would be difficult to enroll him in a program because he would deny that he is an alcoholic.

An interesting feature of this case is the apparent relationship between excessive drinking and the break-up of a marriage. My estimate is that about three-fourths of the men and women who drink excessively at The Oasis have a marital problem or have been divorced. If this tavern is at all typical there must be hundreds of thousands (if not millions) of such persons in American taverns and other bars.

In this study we do not have the controls that would enable us to determine whether the excessive drinking or the marital failure came first. One might hypothesize that the marital problems tend to precede the excessive drinking, on the simple theory that most people looking for a marital partner would not deliberately choose to marry an excessive drinker.

The above case was presented in some detail because it contains most of the features seen at The Oasis among the persons who cannot manage their use of alcohol. These features include (a) loss of productive effort by some skilled worker in the "prime of life"; (b) marital problems, with or without divorce; (c) neglect of children;* (d) damage to the community in the form of nonsupport of wife and children, unpaid bills, etc.; and (e) damage to the person himself. This young worker was a big likable guy—or at least he must have been likable earlier in life before he had deteriorated so much.

This man had spent time in the armed forces, in fact he once said that he had started drinking while stationed in Japan. This history of military service and its related drinking is also rather typical of the men who use alcohol excessively at The Oasis.

"An Old Guy Who Drinks Too Much"

An entirely different pattern of excessive drinking is represented by an old man of seventy who gets drunk regularly at The Oasis. Mike used to work in a paper factory, a major industry in the state. He never advanced very far in his job, that is, he worked all his life on the production line. He is now retired and lives with a sister in the area of The Oasis, but most of his life he lived farther north, where the paper industry is located. In a sense, then, he is stranded socially at the present time; most of his old drinking buddies and his old taverns are "up north."

Every month, when Mike receives his social security check, he goes on a two- or three-day "binge"; he gets "high" every day, wants to buy everybody a drink, plays the jukebox, and has a big time. "Have a drink on old Mike," he will say. "The eagle is flying today."

On the second or third day the proprietor suggests to Mike that he put a little money away for beer at the end of the month. This reminds Mike that the binge can't last forever and he usually deposits $10 to be held for him "when I need it." This usually turns out to be about the middle of the month.

As the month drags on and Mike gets thirstier, he begins to tap various sources that help to see him through until his next check comes. One source is the neighborhood barber shop where he has a drawing account of $5 a month, to be repaid from his next social security check. He also taps his sister for small amounts when he gets desperate for a drink.

People at The Oasis don't worry about Mike and his "drinking

---

*I did not have direct evidence of this in the above case but it was reported by other customers.

problem"; they don't even bother to call him an alcoholic. One of the younger men put it this way: "Let the old bastard have his fun. What else has he got left? He can't go to bed with a woman any more—hell, all he can do is eat and drink. I'd get drunk too if I was that old." This expresses rather well the attitude of most of the customers toward Mike's "drinking problem."

An interesting feature of Mike's drinking is a layer of his personality that emerges when he gets intoxicated: he becomes a bitter anti-Semite and a vicious racist in his attitude toward American black people. Several times when he has been drunk he has said: "Hitler had some good ideas, you know. He took care of the Jews. That's what we should do with the niggers in this country." Mike does not express these attitudes when he is sober.

Once when Mike was drunk his racial talk became so offensive that one of the younger customers told him off. "Shut your goddamn mouth," he said. "You're getting to be a dirty old man." Mike left the bar and went home at that point.

There are undoubtedly hundreds of thousands of elderly drinkers somewhat like Mike to be found in the taverns of America. To some extent they represent the anomic feeling that a great many elderly Americans have: they know they are not revered and they view the expression "golden years" as a cruel joke.

The words "alcoholic" or "problem drinker" do not seem appropriate for elderly drinkers such as Mike, and I have never heard anybody at The Oasis use such expressions in referring to heavy drinkers of his age. The reason is simple; Mike has nobody to hurt: he doesn't have a job to perform any more, his wife is dead, his children are grown up, and since he doesn't drive a car he is no hazard to the community.

If Mike were receiving public welfare rather than social security his drinking would be bitterly resented by most of the customers at The Oasis, but they feel he has the right to spend his retirement income as he sees fit. This is one reason to support an income maintenance program such as social security rather than a welfare program such as old age assistance.

Conclusion

In looking at the excessive drinkers at The Oasis it seems quite clear that the men use a very simple test as to whether or not a man is an alcoholic: does he hold his job? If he can't work because of alcohol then he can be called an "alcoholic." This, of course, would not apply to an elderly man who was retired. This definition of an alcoholic reflects the view of these men that their most basic role in society is to work and provide for their families.

It would seem that the above definition is too narrow; it ignores the damage done to marriage and children from excessive drinking. It also ignores the damage to the community from the driver who has had too much to drink.

In discussing female alcoholics it seems that the customers of The Oasis apply two tests: (1) does the woman neglect her children as the result of excessive drinking; and (2) does she become sexually promiscuous when drinking?* Here, again, the damage which excessive drinking may do a marriage is not spelled out, but it may be implied in the above—namely, that no husband would tolerate a wife who neglected her children or was sexually promiscuous.

There is another type of excessive drinker that The Oasis patrons do not label "alcoholics": these are pathetic types who show up briefly at the tavern from time to time and then disappear.† The attitude of the customers toward these heavy drinkers seems to be similar to that expressed toward Mike: what else have these pathetic characters to live for? Implied in this attitude is the idea that these persons have nothing to contribute to society, hence their excessive drinking represents no tragedy, that is, there is no loss to anybody.

One certainly emerges from The Oasis with the conviction that drinking has to be judged *by the results.* It is not the amount of alcohol consumed, it is the end result of the drinking that counts.

TAVERNS AND ALCOHOLISM

I once attempted to get the proprietor of The Oasis to give me a definition of "an alcoholic." To my surprise he more or less rejected the notion that there are persons who fit the label "alcoholic." Since

---

*Note that they do not concern themselves about male promiscuity, only female.

†See a later section of this chapter for a description of some of these people.

the proprietor has always seemed to be a very intelligent observer of the human condition, his reluctance to discuss the alcoholic and the problem of alcoholism was impressive.

In another blue-collar tavern I studied in a different community, the proprietor was also reluctant to discuss the definition of an "alcoholic." "I don't know what you're talking about," he said. "Sure, some of the people who come in here drink too much, but what the hell—they also drive too fast, eat too much, and screw around too much. There are lots of ways to ruin your life. These people just prefer alcohol."

Is this the attitude of the tavern industry toward alcoholism, a problem that some observers call "the number one public health problem in the United States"?[4] Does the liquor industry really think that by ignoring alcoholism the problem will go away?

It is my belief that nobody could study a tavern such as The Oasis without concluding that alcoholism (or excessive drinking) is a serious problem in the United States. This is not intended as a criticism of the management of The Oasis, which is probably superior to most taverns in the state.

It is a frightening prospect to sit in The Oasis (or any other bar) and watch intoxicated persons go to the parking lot and head for the highways. In this state it has been concluded that approximately 50 percent of all fatal car accidents involve excessive drinking.[5] One can readily understand this if he studies any bar or any tavern for any length of time.

One related problem is the failure of bars and taverns to observe the state law about serving persons who are obviously "under the influence of alcohol." The writer has yet to find a bar or tavern in the state that really enforces this law. One reason seems to be that the state does not suspend liquor licenses or impose fines for violation of this law. In sharp contrast, the management of The Oasis is rigorous in not selling beer or liquor to minors, also not permitting them to be in the tavern unless accompanied by a parent or guardian. I have frequently seen drunks served liquor or beer at The Oasis but I have never seen a minor served beer or liquor there.

Another reason why intoxicated persons are served in The Oasis is that refusal to serve often precipitates trouble: if it is a regular customer he will very likely take his business elsewhere, and if it is a stranger he may start a fight if the bartender refuses him a drink.*

I once discussed the problem of serving intoxicated persons with the operator of The Oasis. He considered it a very difficult problem. "Look," he said, "if a minor walks in, I can ask to see his I.D. card. This is an official document that tells me whether or not this person is entitled to be served in my tavern. But when I suggest to a customer that he has had enough to drink he wants to know who in the hell I am to make this judgment. I don't have any blood test or any other way of determining when a person is intoxicated. Some of the guys who come in here can hold a hell of a lot of liquor and not get into any trouble."

The proprietor does try to "bar" customers who habitually "cause trouble" at The Oasis, but it is a public place and legally he has to serve all persons of legal age—unless they are clearly intoxicated.[6]

The problem of serving intoxicated persons in taverns and other bars was argued in 1970 before the Wisconsin Supreme Court: "A century old doctrine absolving tavern-keepers from civil liability for damages caused to others by persons who become drunk should be abandoned, the Supreme Court was told today."[7] This was part of a damage suit in which a woman was trying to recover damages for injuries suffered in a car accident in which she was injured. She argued that the driver (her husband) had been served alcohol in a tavern after he was clearly intoxicated. "The appeal precipitated a rash of briefs to be filed with the Supreme Court in the case by the Wisconsin Tavern Keepers' Association, Tavern League of Wisconsin, Wisconsin Restaurant Association, Wisconsin State Hotel Association, and the Wisconsin State Brewers' Association."[8] The court ruled in favor of the tavern.

One of the serious dysfunctions of the average bar or tavern is its tolerance of the excessive drinker—the future alcoholic. In a very real sense the tavern (or bar) provides a "cover" or "protective coloring" for the man or woman who is already drinking too much and in danger of becoming an alcoholic.[9] This can readily be observed at The Oasis on almost any day or night.

*Since beginning this study in 1963 I have collected several news stories about bartenders who were shot by persons who had been refused a drink.

There is a process of decline or disenchantment when a regular (not a transient) patron of the tavern begins to drink excessively:

1. At first the individual is amusing to the other customers. "You should have seen Jerry last night—he was very funny!"

2. In the second stage the excessive drinker begins to be obnoxious. "Somebody is going to clobber that guy if he doesn't watch his mouth." As a matter of fact, such persons are sometimes beaten up physically during this stage of the decline cycle.

3. The regular patrons begin to avoid the offender: he is excluded from their circle of social interaction.

4. The excessive drinker either reforms (begins to control his drinking) or he disappears from this particular tavern.

I have observed this process several times during the period of this study.

Aside from the damage to the lives of the people who drink too much, there is the constant problem of these persons walking (or staggering) out of bars or taverns and getting behind the wheel of an automobile. In the lawsuit cited above the attorney for the plaintiff claimed that "drunken drivers" are responsible for 25,000 deaths and at least 800,000 automobile accidents annually in the United States. At the moment there is no solution to this problem in this state. It would seem that an intoxicated person who can still walk will be served at The Oasis and most other bars in the state.

THE PARADE OF CHARACTERS AT A TAVERN BAR

One of the fascinating features of a tavern is the parade of characters that come and go. These persons are not regulars at The Oasis: they are fringe patrons who show up for a few days, or a few weeks (sometimes a few months), and then disappear. Often they are never seen again—or they may suddenly reappear. They are not really accepted by the regulars but are tolerated if they do not cause "too much trouble." In a sense these floaters—most of whom are excessive drinkers—provide a sort of continuous floor show for the regular patrons and the proprietor.

The Man Who Loved His Dog

One of these persons was a man who no longer loved his wife (with whom he still lived) but had transferred all of his affection to his dog, with whom he slept. "I love that big sonofabitch,"* he would say. "He won't go to bed until I get home—he sits in the garage and waits for me. If I've had too much, he can tell and then he growls like hell." He stopped to order another brandy.

"That big bastard is smart," he continued. "I used to drink at a tavern near my house and that damn dog would come up there after me. He would sit by the door until somebody opened it, than he would slip in and work his way around the bar until he found me. Then he would grab me by the ankle and keep tugging until I went home. I kid you not. That sonofabitch would hold on until I got up and left with him. I finally had to stop drinking at that place."

"Did you try teaching the dog to drink—give him beer or brandy to see if he liked it?"

"I tried that. The sonofabitch is a teetotaler—he won't touch a drop."

"What does your wife think about your sleeping with the dog?"

"Piss on her. I've had that dog since he was a pup and I love that big sonofabitch."

One noon this man came into the tavern and had obviously been drinking heavily. His right hand was swathed in a large surgical dressing.

I asked him what had happened.

"My dog bit me last night," he said. "I had to go to the emergency room and have 12 stitches put in." He ordered a brandy.

"Why did he bite you?"

"Well, I had a hell of a snootful when I got home and he growled like hell all the time I was getting ready for bed. In coming out of the bathroom I fell and the big sonofabitch sank his teeth into my right hand. It took me fifteen minutes to pry his mouth open and get my damn hand out."

'Did you take the dog to the veterinarian?"

"Yeah."

---

*The dog was reported to be a springer spaniel weighing 120 pounds.

"What did he say?"

"He said I would either have to quit drinking or get rid of the dog."

"What are you going to do?"

"I had the big sonofabitch put to sleep this morning."

He ordered another brandy and began to sob; it was obvious that the entire episode had been very disturbing.

"Are you going to get another dog?"

"No—never. I loved that sonofabitch too much." Then he added:

"But I might get myself a different woman."

This man disappeared from the tavern and was not seen again.

One Dozen Roses

St. Patrick's Day always calls for a big celebration at The Oasis, even though most of the regular patrons are not of Irish descent. Drinking is heavier than usual on this day, Irish songs are played on the juke box, green decorations are put out—and one year green beer was served from the tap. This last was too much. A customer yelled: "Harry, for Christ sake, we don't mind celebrating St. Patrick's Day, but please don't serve any more green beer—it makes me hate the Irish."

One year the St. Patrick's Day celebration lasted all week. Two men, neither one Irish, were at the tavern every day, from noon until closing, singing Irish songs and buying everybody a drink.

As the week progressed (or deteriorated) it became clear that the one man's wife had died a few months earlier, and the friend was helping the widower "drown his sorrow," as they say at the tavern.

It seems that the man whose wife had died had a duck farm—he grew ducks for the commercial market. It developed that the widower had a habit of singing to the ducks when he fed them in the evening. He discussed this at great length one day with his drinking partner. "Do you think I'm nuts for singing to my ducks?" he asked his buddy. "I sing to them every night when I put out their feed. Do you think that's right?"

His companion, ordering another drink, assured him that ducks—

especially *young* ducks—liked to be sung to. In fact, some ducks wouldn't grow if you *didn't* sing to them.

The widower was not so sure. "I started singing to them after my wife died," he said. "Maybe I *am* crazy—sometimes I think so."

Later, the man whose wife had died began to talk to me. He was upset by something that had happened at the plant where he worked. "There is this nice woman in the same department where I work. I guess we have worked there together for about fifteen years now. Anyhow, when my wife was dying she asked about her every day, and once she even came to the hospital. And when my wife finally died—she had cancer—this woman sent the most beautiful card you ever saw."

He stopped to buy a drink for himself and everybody at the bar. Then he continued:

"A couple weeks ago this lady asked me how my children were getting along and all at once I decided to do something—I made up my mind to send that woman one dozen roses for being so nice to me.

"That night, on my way home from work, I stopped at that fancy flower store on State Street and told the man to send that woman the most beautiful roses he had—one dozen—and I didn't care how much they cost."

He finished his beer, ordered another one, and then told the rest of the story.

"You know what happened? Two days later this woman's husband was watching for me at the parking lot at the plant. When I drove in he came over to my car and said if I didn't stop chasing his wife he would report me to the police—then he walked away."

The widower was almost in tears at this point.

"I swear before God that I never touched that woman. I never saw her except at work. I just sent the roses to tell her how nice she had been to me—and now her husband claims I did something bad. Do you think I was wrong for sending them roses?"

I said no, that the woman would understand, even though her husband did not.

After another beer he and his buddy departed to feed the ducks.

They had decided that this evening they would *both* sing to the ducks, using only Irish songs.

The Air-Conditioned Dog House

A man stopped in at the tavern one day and told the following story. The proprietor said later that he did not know who this man was.

"Last year I decided to build a nice new dog house for my dog. My wife doesn't like dogs and I keep him out in the back yard most of the time.

"Anyhow, I started building this dog house in the basement and it was really nice—I put insulation all over the sides and roof, laid linoleum on the floor, and it really looked good."

He stopped long enough to order a double shot of brandy.

"Well, about that time my wife and I had a helluva big fight. She thought I should be remodeling the kitchen instead of spending all of my time on this dog house.

"I got so damn mad that I decided to enlarge the dog house and make it big enough for me and the dog both. I didn't plan now on putting it in the back yard—the damn thing got to be too big to get through the basement door.

"Well, sir, when it was all done it was really something. I put a little air conditioner in the thing and a portable TV and it's real nice."

Another brandy. "I watch the ball games down there with my dog—it's cool in the summer and warm in the winter."

"What does your wife think of all this?"

'She's mad as hell—but that's nothing new."

It would be possible to do an entire book on the transient "characters" who have appeared and disappeared at The Oasis during the period of this study. Most of these people drink too much, and most of them have suffered some tragedy in their life. They apparently "wear out" their welcome at one tavern and then move on to another.

A RAINY AFTERNOON AT THE OASIS

If you want to see a tavern such as The Oasis when the action is at its peak, drop in some weekday afternoon when it is raining and the men have had to stop work. They will begin to cluster at noon for lunch, and if it is raining hard the beer and liquor will begin to flow—the men can sense there will be no more work that day. Some of them will still be drinking at the tavern when it closes at 1 A.M.

One rainy afternoon I heard the following exchange:

"Have another drink."

"Can't—have to go give blood for a buddy."

'Have another drink and give your buddy a lift."

This was a Thursday afternoon and the weather forecast predicted rain for Friday also. Some of the men were elated by the prospect. "This stuff looks like it will last through tomorrow," one of them said. "Let's really tie one on." He was referring to the fact that they would not have to be sober until Monday morning—almost four days.

As the rain continued the tavern began to fill up and by 4 P.M., when I left, the place was really jumping. The juke box was playing, some of the men were dancing with two young women who had strayed into the place, card games were in progress, men were waiting their turn for the pool table, and the bartender had to send for extra help. It was quite an afternoon.

10 Politics, Race, and Religion

"I think the bastards are all crooked."

Statement about politicians by a customer at The Oasis

INTRODUCTION

During the period of this study a number of major issues confronted the United States: the war in Vietnam, assistance to other countries, pollution of the environment, poverty and welfare programs, the exploration of outer space, the status of women, the revolt of youth against "the establishment," and the massive problems faced by blacks and other minority groups. In this chapter we will look at these issues through the eyes of the men and women at The Oasis. A tavern provides a good listening post from which to follow the shifting mood of a particular segment of the population. Almost any observer, for example, sitting in The Oasis during the presidential campaign of 1968, could have predicted that the Democrats were in trouble—their traditional blue-collar faithfuls were being wooed successfully by George Wallace and Richard Nixon. The memory of Franklin D. Roosevelt was no longer enough to assure the votes of labor; the men were now affluent and worried about problems other than unemployment and the right of collective bargaining.

In this chapter, then, we explore the view of the blue-collar elite as they look out of their favorite tavern at the world around them.

POLITICAL PARTIES

In the English studies of the affluent blue-collar worker by the Goldthorpe research group, it was concluded that most of the men

170

in their sample remained loyal to the Labour Party even after they had moved up to a higher income bracket.[1] Those men felt that the Labour Party was really the only political party representing "the working class." For the United States, both Arthur Kornhauser et al. and Bennett M. Berger have concluded that auto workers remain loyal to the Democratic party even though they become affluent and move to suburbia.[2]

This study, a decade later than the two cited above, comes to a different conclusion: the blue-collar elite in this sample no longer profess any loyalty to the Democrats or to any other political party. They have become "swing" voters, casting their ballot according to the mood of the moment. If they reveal any political movement it is to the right, toward Nixon-Ford conservatism and/or Wallace reactionism. They are quite disillusioned with political liberalism, feeling that it has failed to deliver on its promises.

Actually, the prevailing political mood of these men during the 1960s was one of deep cynicism: they felt that all of America's statesmen were dead and that the country was being run by a bunch of political hacks.*

The former Democrats at the tavern seem to be in mourning for John F. Kennedy—not Franklin D. Roosevelt. Lyndon Johnson never was able to spark any enthusiasm in these men. "The bastard tried hard enough," one carpenter said, "he just wasn't smart enough. Running a ranch and running the United States are two different things."

In 1968 the men were in a mood to vote *against* the Democrats rather than *for* the Republicans. As one man put it, "Let's throw the rascals out and put in a new bunch of rascals."

Some of the men in 1968 were drifting toward George Wallace. This was primarily a reaction to riots in two urban centers in the state. One man said: "I probably won't vote for Wallace but the sonofabitch has some good ideas. I think he would straighten out some of those black bastards like Rap Brown and Stokely Carmichael."

---

*This cynicism is analyzed in a later section of this chapter.

The above remarks apply primarily to national politics. On a state and local level the men vote for the man, not the party.

In considering why my findings are different from those of Korn-hauser and Berger, the following facts need to be considered: the interviews in this study were done approximately a decade later than those of Berger and Kornhauser; the auto workers' union, used in the previous studies, has always been a "liberal" and progressive union compared to the craft unions of the construction industry; the auto workers' union has been closely identified with the Democratic party; the urban riots of the 1960s drove many so-called liberals to the political right; and, finally, the Republican party in this particular state has an unusual history in that the state's most glorious era, 1900-1925, was a Republican period—the late Robert M. LaFollette had at that time developed the Progressive party, an offshoot of the Republican party, and as governor pushed through a series of en-lightened labor laws, including the first unemployment compensa-tion law in the country.[3]

INTERNATIONAL POLITICS

During the period of this study one could literally see and feel the growth of a new form of "isolationism" among the blue-collar aristocrats at The Oasis. The tragic war in Vietnam was undoubtedly the most important (or the most obvious) factor related to this trend but there were other forces operating as well.

During the late 1960s the village in which The Oasis is located inaugurated the practice of displaying the American flag along the main street on the day of any military funeral. This meant that the residents were periodically reminded of the death of another local boy in Vietnam: they saw the flags on the main street as they drove to work in the morning and on their way home at night.

Once the purpose of this flag display was understood by the general public, hundreds of flags were put out on military funeral days by individual home owners. The mass effect was impressive. The village took on the appearance of the Fourth of July or the old-fashioned Decoration Day whenever another boy killed in Viet-nam was buried.

By coincidence the tavern is located beside a cemetery, so that often persons can sit at the bar and watch one of these military funeral processions go by. I was present at the tavern on several occasions when this happened.

On one particular day they were burying a very popular young man who had only graduated from the local high school the year before and had been killed by a land mine his first week in Vietnam. The funeral was a large one. Flags were flying all over town as the long line of cars came down the main street from the church and turned left toward the cemetery, passing directly in front of the bar at The Oasis. The tension inside the tavern was almost tangible as the cars passed slowly by, each car with a small American flag sticking up from the right front fender.

For a minute or so nobody spoke. Then a man said: "I guess they are burying that Jones boy today."

One man was visibly shaken as he watched the funeral go by. He did not speak until the last car has passed. "I'll be a goddamn sonofabitch!" he said. "For Christ's sake how long are they going to let that slaughter go on over there? The whole goddamn country of South Vietnam is not worth the life of one American boy, no matter what the hell our politicians try to tell us. I'm damn sick and tired of watching those funerals go by."

He ordered another glass of beer and was silent for a minute or two. Then he said: "I was in World War II and that was bad enough, but by God we at least knew what we were fighting for and who we were fighting against. But that poor kid they're burying today—what the hell chance did he have to know why he was sent halfway around the world to fight for a goddamn country he never heard of? It's a goddamn shame and I get sick to my stomach every time another one of our kids gets killed over there."

He put on his hat, picked up his change and headed for the door. As he went out he turned and said: "I'm going home and get drunk. I can't stand this crap anymore."

It was an impressive scene; one could hardly imagine a good film or television director staging it more effectively.

The other customers said very little at this time; they were obviously impressed by the deep feeling being expressed by this man as the military funeral went by.

Some thirty-five young boys from this village and the surrounding communities were killed in Vietnam during the period of this study.[4] Newspaper stories, radio announcements, and television news films kept reminding the local citizens of the terrible price being paid for the Vietnam war.

Another factor pushing the men at The Oasis toward isolationism was the anti-American feeling expressed by demonstrators all over the world: in Japan, Venezuela, India, and even England. Most of these countries had received massive aid from the United States in recent decades.

When one of these incidents would flare up in the news a wave of anger and consternation would sweep over the men at the tavern. You would hear comments of this sort: "Jesus Christ, they attacked the American Embassy in Rome—why those dirty bastards. We went over there in World War II and got the goddamn Germans off their backs and then we fed them for about ten years so they wouldn't starve to death—and now they're yelling 'Yankee Go Home.' I say to hell with those bastards from now on."

An intense feeling of resentment was obvious in these men when anti-American riots were reported from India. "As much food as we have sent over there," one man said, "how in the hell can they feel that way against us?" Another man said: "I think we should stop sending food and limit our aid to birth control pills and rubber condoms—that's what those bastards need most anyhow."

I once took a professor from India to The Oasis and introduced him to several of the regular customers. They questioned him at length about the anti-American demonstrations in India. His reply was that these incidents were provoked by the Communist party in India and did not represent the feelings of the average person. This made the men at the tavern feel a little better about the situation in India.

Higher taxes were also a factor in the new isolationist trend at The Oasis. Income taxes, sales taxes, real estate taxes—all of these increased during the 1960s, and the blue-collar aristocrats were well aware that foreign aid (military and other types) was a factor in pushing up federal taxes. "I wouldn't mind so much if I thought it was doing any good," one man said. "But I think it's money down the drain and that burns the hell out of me."

Most of the men at the tavern have little enthusiasm for the space program. They feel that it has too much priority over domestic needs. "I can't see what is so goddamn urgent about putting a man on the moon," a plumber remarked. "Here we have our lakes and rivers going to hell and they say there's no money to do anything about it. Why is the moon so damn important?"

Most of these men believe that our military ventures in Korea and Vietnam were costly mistakes, that billions of dollars and thousands of American lives were expended on hopeless causes. As one man put it: "I think we had to fight Hitler and we sure as hell had to put the Japanese in their place after Pearl Harbor, but by God I couldn't see Korea and I sure as hell can't see Vietnam. Asia belongs to the Asians and we ought to let them fight it out over there." Another man said: "The trouble is, we're trying to be a policeman for the whole damn world and it's not working."*

It seems that most of the men at The Oasis are in favor of economic aid to nations that are friendly to the United States; they don't mind sending them food, medicine, birth control supplies, heavy machinery, and the like. They are bitter about our use of "American boys" to fight all over the globe and also about economic aid to nations that are friendly to the Soviet Union.

The men at The Oasis are not pacifists. They believe in military preparedness and they accept the fact that war may be necessary if the United States is attacked, but they do not see (or believe) that an attack on South Korea or South Vietnam is an attack on the United States. "All of those countries are corrupt as hell," one man said, "and it doesn't make a goddamn bit of difference to us whether South Vietnam wins or North Vietnam wins—there's no democracy over there anyhow."

Another reason why the men at the tavern are wary about military intervention abroad is that they lack faith in the judgment of their leaders in such situations. "Look at the Bay of Pigs disaster in Cuba," a carpenter observed. "That should never have been attempted at all. And that was Kennedy, who was a helluva lot smarter than Johnson or Nixon will ever be."

The men feel that Truman made the wrong decision in sending troops into Korea, that both Kennedy and Johnson were wrong about Vietnam, and that Nixon had no better judgment than his predecessors in the White House. "How the hell would he know what do do?" one man said. "He's just a small town boy from California who had a good television manager in the last campaign—

---

*When a statement represents the dominant sentiment at The Oasis it usually goes unchallenged. But if a minority position is advanced, vigorous dissent will be heard. Very few isolationist statements have been challenged during this study.

and was lucky enough to line up with Eisenhower several years ago."

The tavern customers also have no faith that their representatives in Congress have any special insight into foreign military problems. Comments such as the following are often heard: "If those guys are so damn smart, why did they vote all the money and the troops for Vietnam? They put all the blame on Johnson, but the president can't start a war all by himself—he has to have the money and Congress controls that."

If you follow this line of reasoning—that is, if you don't trust your political leaders to make the correct decisions about military intervention overseas—then you retreat to some sort of isolationism. "I say let's be prepared at all times but wait for them to attack us—then knock the hell out of them. That's how we handled the Japanese and that's how we should handle all the rest of those yellow bastards."

LOCAL POLITICS

On a local level a ten-year struggle has developed between the "old" residents and the "new" residents for control of the city government. On one side are aligned the elderly people (some of them retired farmers) and the original blue-collar residents, while on the other side are the middle-class couples who have purchased expensive homes in the newly developed areas, plus the new white-collar apartment dwellers.

Two incidents of the 1960s illustrate the conflict between the above groups. In the first one, the city council was debating whether or not to force home owners in an expensive wooded area to install sidewalks. The owners argued that the sidewalks would not only require that trees be cut down, but that in addition the "woodsy" nature of the area would be negatively affected. The owners went on to point out that no real hazards for children were involved and cited the examples of two expensive suburbs in the area that did not require sidewalks.

The city council members from the older sections of the town were adamant: "we had to have sidewalks and you are no better than we are . . . all towns have sidewalks . . . etc."

Actually, it was primarily a contest to see who was running the city. The sidewalks were voted in.

In a discussion of this matter at The Oasis, the following comment was made: "Well, I see that the new bastards* don't want sidewalks. Well, that's just too damn bad. They think they can come in here and take over the place. Thank God the city council told them where to get off."

In the other incident an addition to the high school had been approved, after much struggle, and a debate developed as to what side of the school to build on: there was a rather large area to the west that might have been used for the addition, but this would have seriously damaged the aesthetic approach to the school. Furthermore, the architects felt that the addition could be fitted better to the existing structure if the new section was placed to the east.†

In building to the east, however, additional land would have to be purchased; a very fine baseball diamond, with permanent bleachers and lights, would have to be demolished; and the varsity football field would have to be moved. The final decision was to leave the campus on the west as it was and to build on the east. In this battle, the middle class won.

Many comments were heard by blue-collar patrons at The Oasis. "Big Joe" is speaking:

"Did you see what the new bastards did the other night in planning the new addition to the high school? They had about an acre of land vacant on one side of the school so what did they do? They tore up the best damn high school baseball diamond in the state—one that had lights, grass infield, plenty of seats, and everything. I remember when they passed the hat to pay for those lights and I chipped in a few bucks and so did some of you guys.

"Now these new people that just moved in, they're running everything and they don't know anything about what happened ten or fifteen years ago—like the building of that baseball diamond. And, furthermore, they don't care. They're taking over the whole place, school board and everything."

'Big Joe" was expressing a very common point of view on the part of the people in town who have lived there twenty or thirty years

---

*The speaker is referring to the home owners in a newly developed area.

† I was a member of the advisory building committee and attended several school board meetings involving the new addition.

and can remember when it was a small village catering largely to blue-collar families and the surrounding rural areas. These people are quite right when they speak of an "invasion" of their town; almost all of the rapid population growth in the past ten years has been the white-collar overflow from the adjacent metropolitan community.

The problems in this community are typical of small towns that find themselves in the path of metropolitan sprawl. I once asked a patron at the tavern if he did not think Lakeside would be better off if it were annexed to Metropolis. He almost choked on his beer.

"For Christ sake, Doc," he exclaimed, "you must be out of your mind. I think that crazy campus down there is beginning to get to you."

I asked him what his objections were to annexation.

"Very simple," he said. "All government is crooked, but in a small town like this the crooks are small—they don't steal as much, they are easier to watch—and they're easier to catch because they're not too smart."

He stopped to order another beer.

"Now if we annex to Metropolis, we'll be up against the big crooks, the smart ones, and they'll be too much for us. I'm against it."

POVERTY AND WELFARE PROGRAMS

In the "most affluent society in the world" one of the acute issues of the 1960s was that of poverty and programs to alleviate it. How do the blue-collar aristocrats view the poor? Do they sympathize with the less fortunate members of "the working class?"

The answer seems to be no: they feel that welfare recipients are lazy, that they already receive more help than they need, and that a lot of them are "chiselers." Social workers are viewed as "do gooders" who are too easy on the welfare clients.

The following tavern discussion is typical. The speaker is an elderly man but his comments received approval by the younger men at the bar.

"I'm 78 years old—born in 1891. I was a truck driver all my life, hauling coal. I worked hard—you get awful dirty hauling coal all day, loading and unloading it.

"My wife and I raised ten kids—with no help from anybody. I'm awful proud of that."

He stopped to order a glass of beer and then continued. You could tell that he was lonely and wanted to talk.

"Even during the depression we never asked for relief. Had to tighten our belt sometimes but never took any relief.

"Hell, it's different today. Now they go on welfare. I know a farmer who offered a man $200 a month, plus a house to live in, and the man turned it down. Said he could do better than that on the welfare. I don't think that's right."

After a pause the old man looked around the bar and said: "This is my birthday and I'm sort of celebrating. Could I buy everybody a drink?"

The young men at the bar said no, they would buy *him* a drink, which they did. He went away very happy. Nobody knew who he was; his generation was dead.

I was curious whether any of the younger men at the bar would challenge the old man's views on welfare, but none of them did. Is $200 a month "and a house" enough to raise a family on in the 1960s? Some of the men at the bar that day earn $300 a week when they get overtime.

Should our welfare policy force men to work for less than a living wage? Wouldn't that produce cheap labor that might threaten our entire wage structure? Nobody at the bar posed any of these questions.

When "$200 a month" is mentioned, people at The Oasis seem to forget about inflation. The older ones immediately begin to talk about how they lived on "fifty bucks a month" during the depression of the 1930s.

"I remember we used to eat beans seven times a week, but by God we never went on welfare."

"Do you think people can do that today?" I asked one man.

"Yes, by God, I do," he replied. "I think there's honest work for those willing to work—but most of them are too goddam lazy. They would rather sit on their ass and take a hand-out."

"What about their children?"

"Well, that's different. Kids have to be taken care of—but I'd sure as hell take them away from the parents."

Assuming that attitudes of this sort are fairly typical of the blue-collar elite, the problem of developing any rational, humane welfare program becomes almost impossible. At almost any point some "cheap" politician can usually sabotage the program by spewing out the stereotype "welfare chiseler."

In his classic study, *The Other America*,[5] Michael Harrington points out that middle-class people seldom see or come in contact with the poor in modern America. This is, indeed, true, but it is also true of the affluent blue-collar workers. In the five years of this study, for example, only one welfare recipient was a regular patron of this tavern, and only for a relatively short period.* Thus, at work and at play, these blue-collar elite are isolated from the poor and the unfortunate. They would literally have to go out of their way to understand the problems of the underprivileged in our society. Very few, if any, are willing to make this effort.

CAMPUS PROTESTS

During the 1960s violence erupted several times on the state university campus in nearby Metropolis. The national guard was called upon to restore order and to keep the university open. Considerable damage was done, not only on the campus, but also to adjacent business property. The long series of events was climaxed by a massive bombing that killed one person and destroyed over a million dollars of campus property. National leftwing student groups, such as the SDS,† were active on the campus during these years.

The men at The Oasis were shocked and angered by the campus riots. "Jesus Christ!" a truck driver said, "what in the hell is wrong with them crazy bastards down there? They have the best goddamn university in the country and all they do is raise hell. I don't get it." Another man said: "I think we should get our shotguns and go down there some night and teach those bastards a lesson." (This actually happened in 1970 when a group of university students were attacked in New York City by some construction workers during an anti-war demonstration.[6])

---

*This excludes the elderly social security pensioners and persons on unemployment compensation or industrial compensation.

†"Students for a Democratic Society."

The men at the tavern could not understand why the university could not maintain order by dismissing the students involved in the disturbances. "What in the hell is wrong down there?" a carpenter asked me. "If you guys can't handle those characters I think we should get somebody in there who can."

Some of the men at The Oasis felt that the president of the university should be fired and that the board of regents should "take over" the campus.

When the Kent State tragedy occurred there was very little sympathy for the four students who were shot by the Ohio National Guard. "Those kids knew goddamn well that those guns were loaded—why in the hell didn't they clear out when told to?," a painter asked.[7]

A man who had served in the national guard at one of the local riots said this: "One of these days somebody is going to get shot on this campus too. Those kids call you anything they can think of—and the girls are worse than the boys." A policeman who had been involved in a serious riot on the campus said: "They tried to grab me by the nuts and called me names like 'cocksucker.' One girl reached into a green bag—the kind they usually carry books in—took out a rotten egg and threw it in my face."

It was apparent at the tavern during the 1968 presidential campaign that student riots were causing the blue-collar workers to move to the political right. The Chicago disturbances in particular, during the Democratic Convention, had a pronounced effect. Most the men supported Mayor Daley of Chicago in this confrontation. "That Daley may be crooked, but he sure as hell knows how to handle those long-haired bastards," one man said. This seemed to express the general sentiment of the group.

I have never heard any of the blue-collar men at The Oasis express any sympathy or support for the leftwing student movement. They feel that going to college is a great privilege, not a right (as the students claim), and that students should observe the rules established by the authorities or be dismissed. It is a clear-cut issue as far as these men are concerned.

POLLUTION OF THE ENVIRONMENT

One of the few social issues that The Oasis regulars are willing to face is the destruction of the natural environment. Most of these men love to hunt and fish. Furthermore, a substantial percentage of them grew up on farms and have retained a love for the land. In recent years these men have witnessed a dramatic deterioration in the natural world surrounding them. This is best illustrated by what has happened to the beautiful lake near the tavern. "I can remember when that lake was so goddamn clear you could see right to the bottom. Now the weeds and other crap is so thick the birds walk right on top of it." This man, a carpenter, lives on the lakeshore.

Another man said: "Us kids used to swim in that lake all summer. Last year they closed the beach and said it wasn't safe for swimming. Now they're talking about building a swimming pool because the lake is ruined. It's a goddamn shame."

Many of the men belong to conservation groups which sponsor legislation intended to preserve the natural environment, plus screening political candidates for their position on pollution control. One man said: "I don't give a damn about putting a man on the moon. I say let's clean up this planet before we get involved with another one." This seems to represent the feeling of the group.

WOMEN'S LIBERATION

Another of the important movements of the 1960s in the United States was the renewal of the struggle to attain social and economic equality for women.[8] How do the blue-collar elite view this proposed change in their world?

The men at The Oasis view women's liberation with more than alarm—with abhorrence would be more accurate. I asked a welder if he was planning to vote for a woman who was a candidate for the local school board. I pointed out that she was well educated, had been active in numerous community projects, and that she was pretty.

The reply was explosive. "I wouldn't vote for her if she was built like Marilyn Monroe," he said. "The goddamn women are trying to take over this town—they're just like the niggers: give them an inch and they'll take a mile."[9]

He ordered a beer and continued.

"I was up at the high school the night they had that big fight about including a swimming pool in the new addition. Hell, the damn women talked so much the men couldn't even get a word in edgewise.

"Am I going to vote for a woman on the school board? Hell, no. They'd probably paint the whole goddamn place pink or lavender or some other crazy color if they ever got control of the school board."

Some weeks later I pointed out to the welder that the woman candidate had been overwhelmingly elected to the school board; in fact she had the largest plurality of any of those elected.

The welder looked depressed. "Look, Doc," he said, "I can't help it if the goddamn world is going to hell. They should never have given women the right to vote in the first place—that's when all the trouble started."

After a pause he said: "Let's have a drink and forget about the whole goddamn mess. I'll match you for it."

He won the coin toss for the drinks and seemed to feel a little better.

One evening at the tavern a nationally prominent, very militant women's liberationist was on a television network "talk show." The set happened to be turned on and a group of plumbers were watching. The place was relatively quiet until the militant woman referred to men as "chauvinist pigs." At this point the bar exploded.

"I'll be a sonofabitch!" one of the men exclaimed. "Did you hear what that bitch called us?"

Another man nodded. "She's a goddamn man-hater," he said. "I heard her once before—she thinks we should all have our nuts cut off and then women would run the world."

The first plumber was still shocked by what he had seen and heard on the television screen; apparently it was his first exposure to a militant female liberationist. After a minute or two he said: "You know what that woman needs?—a good screw. I think that would make her feel better."

Another plumber in the group shook his head. "I don't think a man could screw her—those gals get their kicks the other way."

At this point one of the men asked the bartender to turn off the TV. "That goddamn woman is spoiling our drinking," he said. The bartender complied.

The wives who come to the tavern have sympathy for the women's liberation movement but they are almost as hostile toward the female militants as the men are. One woman said: "I sure as hell think women get a bum deal, but some of those women on television are nuts—it's just like any other movement: the radicals take over and spoil everything."

I asked her if she thought women could run the world any better than men could.

"I really don't know," she said. "We've never had a chance."

Then she added: "But I don't see how we could run it any worse."

POLITICAL CYNICISM

It is quite evident that these men don't trust politicians—whether they voted for them or not. This attitude of cynicism is generalized to include business leaders and trade union officials. As a matter of fact, it is hard to think of any "big wheels" in our society that these men admire and trust. One exception might be sports figures, such as the professional football stars, but even then there is a trace of cynicism: "hell, those guys only play because of the money."

The source of this pervasive cynicism is not entirely clear to this observer.[10] Some of these men have operated their own businesses at some time in the past and often refer to having been "taken" by some unscrupulous business operator higher in the economic hierarchy.

Most of them were enlisted men in the armed forces in World War II or Korea, and they reflect cynical attitudes toward their commissioned officers: "Christ sake," one man said, "if it hadn't been for the chief petty officers the goddamn Navy would have lost World War II. The damn officers didn't know anything."

There is no idealism left in the trade union movement for these men. They have read too many news stories about dishonest union officials to place any great faith in their union leaders. "It's a goddamn racket, like any other racket," one man said of his union. "You pay your dues and keep your mouth shut and they let you work and that's the whole thing in a nutshell."

The puzzle about the cynicism of these men, at least to this observer, arises from the fact that they have actually done quite well in American society: they are at the top of the blue-collar world and most of them, when questioned, admit that they are well paid for their work. Very few of them report harassment or mistreatment on the job. Most of these men survived World War II without serious injury and a majority of them actually "believed" in the war—that is, they felt that after Pearl Harbor America had no choice but to enter the war.

Why, then, should these men be so cynical? One can understand fatalism and cynicism at the lower-class level, the Americans at the bottom of the socio-economic system. But the men in this study occupy a very nice spot in the system, and one might expect them to be less gloomy in their outlook on life.

The political cynicism of these men is evident in numerous remarks. In the 1968 presidential campaign one man said: "What the hell difference does it make whether Nixon or Humphrey wins— they're both goddamn politicians."

When the state governor pushed through a general sales tax, after campaigning on a *No Sales Tax* platform, one man said: "The sonofabitch is crooked as hell. He knew damn well we had to have a sales tax in this state—the bastard just wasn't honest enough to admit it until he got elected."

When Senator Ted Kennedy was involved in the tragic death of a young woman who had helped in various Kennedy campaigns, the men at The Oasis did not accept Kennedy's public explanation of what had happened. "I think the guy was drunk and needed time to sober up—that's why he didn't report the accident for several hours," a carpenter said. Another man said: "I think there was some hanky-panky going on between Kennedy and that girl. That's why he turned off the main road."

The following hypotheses are offered to account for the cynicism of these men:

Their Age

Most of the men in our group (approximately 80 percent) are forty to sixty years old. If it is true, as some observers claim,[11] that idealism and faith in the future are characteristics of youth, then it follows that the men at The Oasis are beyond the age of belief; they have crossed over into the age of disbelief and doubt.

It is not only the age of these men but also the experiences of this particular generation: the economic crisis of the 1930s destroyed a lot of faith and optimism in these men, as did World War II. They have seen the glittering promises of "peace for our time" fade away, one by one, and it is difficult to raise their hopes again.

Their Pragmatism

If you are a skilled mechanic, as most of these men are, earning a living with your hands, then a thing either works or it doesn't. As one carpenter observed, "When I hang a door, that sonofabitch is either hung right or wrong—there's no two ways about it." White-collar people don't usually operate within such a neat system: did the high school teacher do a good job this semester or not? A bricklayer or a plasterer *knows* whether he is doing a good job or not, whereas some of the rest of us are often not sure.

All of the above means that the men at The Oasis don't care much about theory or promises: "does the damn thing work?," they ask. This attitude tends to make them fatalistic or cynical about government and politics because, as they see it, very few of the programs established by government agencies seem to be very effective.

One interesting exception to the above is the faith and respect most of these men have for state and federal conservation programs. They can actually *see* that the deer herd in Wisconsin is larger today than it was twenty years ago; furthermore, they know this could not have been accomplished without state and federal intervention.

Distrust of "Smooth Talkers"

People who work with their hands tend to view with skepticism and distrust people "who work with their mouths." This feeling extends to businessmen, politicians, preachers, and professors.* These men may revere the written word (although this is less and less true), but they certainly are skeptical of the spoken word.

One way to cut a man down at The Oasis is to refer to him as a "smooth talker."† This means that he may not be too honest—a person you have to watch.

*One man said to me one day: "Goddammit, LeMasters, you talk like a damn politician."

†It is an interesting fact that the two presidents most admired in recent decades by these men, Truman and Eisenhower, were neither one what could be called a "smooth talker."

The Impact of the Mass Media

It is literally true that most of the news in newspapers, news magazines, or on radio and television, is *bad* news: the war in Vietnam in the 1960s, traffic fatalities, tragic fires, murders, etc. If you read or hear or see this negative diet for several decades, as these men have, there tends to be a cumulative effect. This, of course, would not be an experience unique to these men, but it would be a factor in explaining their attitude of cynicism and fatalism toward political figures and public affairs.

This Attitude of Cynicism Simply Reflects the Feelings of Most Americans

It may well be that the political attitudes of these men (and their deep cynicism) are not unique or significantly different from those of any other segment of the American population.

RACE

Except for the war in Vietnam, the most explosive issue of the 1960s for the men at The Oasis was the demand of blacks for equality. The construction unions to which these men belong have always been highly segregated racially—and still are for the most part. This is in sharp contrast to the industrial unions, such as the automobile workers, which have been integrated for decades.

Listening to the men at the tavern, one has the impression that the men are more opposed to racial integration than they are to racial equality. One carpenter put it this way: "I realize that something has to be done for the black bastards, but I sure as hell don't want them living next to me. I don't care to work with them either."

If it were possible, the more liberal men in this group would accept the policy of "separate but equal."

As a matter of fact, the men do not accept blacks as being equal to whites—for one thing they regard blacks as being less intelligent than whites. This attitude is revealed in the following incident: A professional football game was being televised on the tavern set. It was obvious that the best players in the game were black.* A man turned

*Although blacks make up only 10 or 11 percent of the United States population, they constitute 60-80 percent of the professional athletes.

to me at the bar and said: "Did you ever stop to think that there are no nigger quarterbacks? They can run all right—but a white man has to tell them what play it is and what to do."* This, of course, is the last line of defense for white men who in their lifetime have witnessed the almost complete domination of football, basketball, baseball, and track by black athletes.

These men watch sports frequently on television—it is their favorite type of program—and they can't help but see the outstanding ability of black athletes. Watching baseball, they could still, in the 1960s, boast that all of the managers in the major leagues were white.† They could also boast that tennis, golf, swimming, bowling, and skiing were still dominated by whites.

The point here is that it is becoming harder and harder for these men to maintain their self-image as being superior to black men. Militant blacks, such as Rap Brown or Stokely Carmichael, drive these men to thoughts of violence.

"That sonofabitch Carmichael," one man said, "should be taken out and strung up by the nuts."

'That's one party I'd like to be in on," another man said.

When Martin Luther King was assassinated, most of the men at the tavern recognized this as a real tragedy—that the country had lost a great man.

"Jesus Christ!" one bricklayer said, "why in the hell did they shoot King? That crazy bastard should have shot Rap Brown—then we could have given the guy a medal."

"Amen," several men at the bar murmured.

Any form of intimacy between white women and black men arouses deep hostility in these men. They often see interracial dating when working on the university campus in nearby Metropolis and they invariably comment on it. "You should have seen the pretty white girl I saw with a big black jigaboo on the campus today. Sonofabitch if I can see how those girls can do it." The speaker was a cement finisher.

---

*Oddly enough, at that time there were no black quarterbacks in professional football but several had won national recognition as quarterbacks at major football colleges. Actually, quarterbacks do not usually call plays in modern football—this is done by the coaching staff.

†There is reason to believe that this barrier will be broken in the 1970s.

The proprietor of The Oasis, Harry, takes a different position on the racial issue. He says that he has been "converted" to believe in equality for all races. "I used to think like the rest of these guys on race," Harry said to me, "but now I know it is wrong. I read a lot of things about Negroes and I now believe they are as good as anybody—maybe better in some things. They are welcome to come in my tavern anytime."*

A devout Roman Catholic, Harry has been persuaded by his church that it is a sin to mistreat a person of another race. This is unusual as I have never heard any other person in the tavern refer to the position of his church in discussing racial issues.

It is obvious that many persons at the tavern still subscribe to folk beliefs about blacks: that they are lazy, not as bright as white people, more childlike, more primitive, more highly sexed, etc. The scientific body of knowledge about human "races" † has penetrated very little, if any, into the blue-collar world.

Finally, if one thinks about the problems of the American Indian, it is clear that the people at The Oasis, like most Americans, are unaware that there is "an Indian problem." A few Indians have come into the tavern during the period of this study and they usually invoke laughter—as if they were a joke. The following dialog is typical:

White customer to bartender: "Paleface buy drink for Chief Longarm."

Bartender to Indian: "That paleface over there want to buy you a drink."

Indian: "Tell him I accept—we smoke peace pipe now."

White customer: "Down the hatch, chief."

Indians are dismissed as being ridiculous by the tavern customers, but blacks are at least taken seriously.

RELIGION

Religion is not a frequent topic of conversation at The Oasis. The

---

*On several occasions black persons did come into the tavern and were served promptly and courteously by the proprietor. This is required by state law, but the law is openly flaunted by some blue-collar taverns.

† I am aware that the very concept of "race" has been under attack in scientific literature.

owner, although quite religious himself, does not encourage the patrons to talk about religion. "They never settle anything," he says, "and it often ends in an argument with some guy getting sore. I have lost some good customers that way."

A rough count of the steady customers at the tavern indicates that 50-60 percent of them are Roman Catholic of German background. This entire region of the state is noted for the fact that its Catholics came from Germany, not Ireland or the other Roman Catholic areas of Europe. The rest of the steady patrons are nominally Protestants (mostly Lutheran), although many of these profess no religious affiliation at the present time.

One has the impression that the men at The Oasis are content to leave religion and the church to women—the men seldom refer to any church activity they have been involved in. A typical comment that reinforces this observation is the following (the speaker is a bricklayer): "The old lady made me get up and go to church Sunday. She said I hadn't been there for over a month."

These men seem to be more nonchurch than antichurch; they do not talk against the church and have no objection to other people (including their wives and their children) being active in it. They just don't care to be deeply involved themselves. This attitude is not limited to the church but reflects their stance toward community organizations in general.

Most of these blue-collar workers seem to be philosophically skeptical in their view of organized religion and its theological base. Working with material things every day, they are not much inclined to believe in "miracles"; they assume that most good things in this world come from "damn hard work," as one man put it. They regard the virgin birth story as a joke. "I sure as hell never knew any virgins to have a baby," one man said. The mystery and mysticism of religious faith leave most of these men cold.

The Catholics and Protestants at the tavern seem to be mutually tolerant: "you let me alone and I'll let you alone." I have never heard a Protestant-Catholic religious argument at The Oasis.

Although Jews seldom patronize this tavern, it seems clear that most of these men are anti-Semitic. They sometimes refer to the cash register as a "Jewish piano."

One Jewish salesman, representing a large brewery, often buys everybody at the bar a drink and has been accepted by the group.

"Moe is not a bad Jew," one man said, "but I sure as hell can't stand most of them."

One facet of resistance to church attendance on the part of these men is their reluctance to "dressing up": they literally hate to wear a coat and necktie. One wife said to me: "I'm going to bury my husband in his T shirt if the undertaker will allow it." The Roman Catholic men have solved the dress problem by wearing a clean sport shirt to church—with a nice sweater in cold weather. Informal attire seems to be less acceptable at Protestant churches, and these men tend to stay home while the wife and children go to church.

Once in a while a violent argument over religion breaks out at The Oasis. When this happens you can see why the topic is usually avoided.

The argument reported here began as a quiet discussion as to whether or not taverns should close for part of Good Friday, usually from noon until 3 P.M.

"I don't see why in the hell taverns should close on Good Friday or any other religious holiday," a man at the bar said. "This is a free country and if I want a drink on Good Friday I don't see why I can't have one."

"It's because Christ was on the cross during those hours," a woman at the bar said.

"Who in the hell knows what hours he was on the cross?" the male customer replied. "Some preacher just picked those hours so he could close the taverns—why didn't he pick 3 to 6 A.M.? That would suit me fine."

"You don't have any religious faith," the woman said. "You'd rather sit here and drink than go to church on good Friday—you don't care that Christ died to save all of us." The woman was getting hostile.

The man was not impressed. "How in the hell do I know what the guy died for?" he said. "All I know was that he got bumped off—I guess he was a troublemaker or something."

At this remark the woman customer snorted with disgust and left the tavern. The man ordered another shot of brandy, and the proprietor suggested that the subject be dropped. The owner decided to close on Good Friday from 1 to 3 P.M.—a period when the tavern would not be very busy anyhow.

During the years of this study the Roman Catholic church was undergoing profound change, but these developments were seldom topics of conversation at The Oasis. One that we recall concerned the demand of priests that they be allowed to marry.

A woman at the bar felt that marriage would be good for priests. "I think it would give them more understanding of life and they would be able to help people more," she said.

A male customer disagreed. "Once those priests discover sex I wouldn't trust them," he said. "I think they should be different from the rest of us—that's what makes them a priest."

The woman laughed. "You're just afraid they'll get some of the stuff you're chasing," she said.

"No, that's not true," the man replied. "I've got all I want—or as much as I can take care of—but I really believe the priests should be virgins. That's the way Christ was, and He understood people."

The woman dropped the argument and went back to drinking beer.

It is an interesting fact that Roman Catholic priests sometimes drop into The Oasis for a beer and sandwich and visit with the customers, but I have never seen a Protestant minister at the tavern.

In some ways the Roman Catholic church seems to be closer to the blue-collar workers at the tavern than the Protestant churches are— besides allowing the men more informal attire, the church service hours at the Catholic church are more flexible; and the church does not object to the use of alcohol (in moderation). Since my background is Protestant I may be romanticizing Roman Catholicism, but the above impressions reflect my observations at The Oasis.

In conclusion, it appears that these men are basically nonreligious. The church exists and they are willing for it to continue existing as long as it makes no great demands on them. One cannot imagine any of these men missing the first day of deer hunting because of some religious function, but then it is hard to imagine their missing the first day of deer hunting for any other reason either.

11 Reflections on the Oasis

"Doc, I hope your book turns
out okay."
*Statement by a regular patron
of The Oasis*

THE NEW GENERATION OF HARD HATS

As this book goes to press, a new generation of construction workers can be seen at The Oasis. Young men with long hair, mustaches, and heavy sideburns (even full beards) are to be seen drinking beer at the bar beside older men with crew cuts and clean-shaven faces. This would have been unthinkable in the 1960s, when "long hairs" were denounced as hippies by the older workers.

A few of these younger men have been to college for a year or two, and all of them have graduated from high school, thus representing a higher level of education that was true of the previous generation of construction workers.

These young men not only wear their hair and beards longer, they are also more liberal in their attitudes toward blacks and other minority groups. "What the hell," one of them said, "those guys have to live too. I don't care if a guy on the job is black. As long as he doesn't try to push me around I won't hassle him either."

One even gets the impression that the younger men are somewhat more liberal on women's liberation than the older workers, but the depth of this change (if it exists) is difficult to gauge. On several occasions in the last year or so heated arguments between younger men over the status of women have been heard at the bar—a new development in itself as the older men didn't think the issue was worth an argument.

Young Men without a Hero

Political trends at The Oasis will be discussed later in this chapter, but it needs to be said here that the younger men at the tavern have no hero: at the moment there is nobody at the national level who speaks for them. At one time John Kennedy or Robert Kennedy might have been their spokesman but now these men are gone and nobody has emerged with their charisma. George McGovern does not inspire them, and it is not clear how much appeal Ted Kennedy has for the new breed of hard hats. In a sense they represent a generation without a leader.

Sexual Norms among the Younger Men

It is difficult to assess how the sexual norms of the younger workers at The Oasis vary from those of the older generation, if indeed there is any difference at all. One has the impression that the new generation is less hostile toward homosexuals and that perhaps the younger men are less promiscuous sexually. Both generations take premarital sex for granted but the new generation seems more inclined to stay with one sexual partner at a time. If this is true it may reflect the "going steady" complex which has been dominant in American high schools since World War II.

Both generations seem to accept extramarital sexual relations for men, but I have the impression that the younger men are less enthralled about the prospect.

Old Veterans Versus New Veterans

I have never heard a young veteran of Vietnam say a good word for that war at The Oasis. This is in sharp contrast to the feelings of the older men toward World War II and constitutes an important part of the generation gap between the two groups. One of the Vietnam veterans expressed his feelings as follows: "It was a goddamn nightmare from the first day to the last. Most of the time you couldn't tell who was fighting who. We got drunk every goddamn night—that was the only way you could stand it." The young veterans have no feeling of having accomplished anything in Vietnam to compensate for the men killed and disabled. This is not true of the men who fought in World War II.

In 1974 the local suburban weekly newspaper ran a feature story of a young man in the village who is a paraplegic from the war in Indochina. The photograph used with the story showed the young man sitting in his wheelchair facing the camera. He tells the reporter that he is bitter because he feels that America should not have been in the war in Asia. This story aroused considerable comment at The Oasis.

Attitudes toward Work

Listening to the new generation of construction workers one gets the impression that the old craftsman type that was described in chapter 2 has more or less disappeared. The younger men are trained in mass production methods—large apartment complex and commercial type construction work—which emphasize speed and daily output rather than individual skill. The new generation does not seem to talk about their work as much; their tavern conversation centers about their softball team or the bowling league. Some of them even talk about golf—a game which held little interest for their elders.

Some of the younger men were socialized to be white-collar workers but dropped out of college for one reason or another and joined the blue-collar elite because of the relatively high wages and the fringe benefits. Psychologically and socially these men are middle classers who happen to be construction workers at the moment. They are quite different from the older farm boys who didn't like farming and struck gold in the building trades during the boom years of the 1950s and the 1960s.

Some of the differences discussed in this section merely reflect age differentials: young guys play softball when old guys have retired to watching sports on television. But beneath the age differentials there are other differences you can feel but find difficult to spell out in words.

DEATH AND DESTRUCTION AT THE TAVERN

During the period of this study several persons at The Oasis suffered death or destruction of some sort. A young worker, for example, only in his early thirties, was killed. Always in a hurry, whether driving his car or on the job, he was killed when he failed to exercise caution while working high above the ground. His entire life had been one of speed and action, and many persons at the tavern had predicted he would never live to be an old man. A participant in numerous brawls at the tavern, this person seemed destined for a short and violent life. Interestingly enough, although this young man had often been the target of unkind remarks at the tavern while alive, I never heard anybody speak negatively of him after his death. As they say at The Oasis, "if you can't say anything good about the dead, then don't say anything."

One of the likable older men at the tavern (his fiftieth wedding anniversary was described in chapter 3) died of cancer during the process of this study. He was in his late seventies at the time of his death, had had a good life, and his departure from this world was accepted with good grace by his friends.

The woman who had once lived in her car in the parking lot of The Oasis died in her early forties before this study was completed. Although an alcoholic, the cause of death was reported to have been a heart attack. At one time she had been hospitalized in a state mental facility but was not living there at the time of her death. Like the young construction worker above, she always seemed to the regular customers to be destined for a short life.

One of the male customers whose wife had left him for another man gradually sank into chronic alcoholism during the years of this study and was eventually admitted to a veteran's facility. A widow attempted to overcome his addiction to the bottle but finally gave up the struggle. This man was well liked at the tavern, and his destruction was viewed with sorrow. He once said to me: "I'm not lucky enough to die young." He felt that his entire life had been one disaster after another.

The woman sometimes referred to at the tavern as The Blonde Bomber (her life story is summarized in chapter 4) seemed on the verge of destruction when last seen at The Oasis. She appeared to be drinking more heavily than usual and tried to take off her clothes one night at the tavern when intoxicated. The proprietor took a dim view of this behavior (he argued that he was not operating a strip joint), and after this episode she was more or less ostracized by most of the regular customers. She and her male partner eventually disappeared from The Oasis and were seen no more.

An insurance man who frequented the tavern (he sold disability policies to blue-collar workers) was jailed for failure to make support payments to his former wife and emerged hating all women. I had never before met a man with the hostility toward women that this man developed in jail. He is consumed with a desire to "get even"— not just with his former wife but with all women. "I want to screw 'em and hurt 'em," he says. It is disturbing to talk with this man in his present state of mind.

THE HOMOGENIZATION HYPOTHESIS

In recent years some observers have postulated that social class lines in modern Western society have become so blurred that distinct life-styles can no longer be discerned at different socio-economic levels. This study tends to support the conclusions of Herbert J. Gans, Bennett M. Berger, Mirra Komarovsky, Gavin Mackenzie, and the Goldthorpe research group in England that the homogenization process, if it exists, is far from complete.[1] Gans is especially emphatic on this point: "the West Enders," he writes, "were not frustrated seekers of middle-class values. Their way of life constituted a distinct and independent working-class subculture that bore little resemblance to the middle-class."[2]

Gans goes on to argue that middle-class social planners and social workers (he calls them caretakers) fail to understand the unique way of life of the blue-collar worker. I have come to the same conclusion on the basis of my observations at The Oasis.

One problem that teachers and social workers face in working with these elite blue-collar couples results from the fact that these husbands and wives adhere to somewhat different values: the women are closer to the middle class than the men are. This is apparent in discussing school programs and/or community recreation programs; the women are child-centered whereas the men are adult-centered.

This male-female difference also shows in their view of marriage: the women prefer the middle-class style of "togetherness" while the men like the sex segregation system reported by Gans and Komarovsky for their blue-collar men. This value stretch between wives and husbands can be very confusing and frustrating to school teachers, social workers, physicians, and other professions attempting to work with these couples.

The three-volume study of affluent blue-collar workers in England after World War II by the Goldthorpe group is emphatic in its rejection of the homogenization process. With some exceptions, such as adoption of the middle-class "togetherness" style of marriage, they conclude that their skilled, well-paid factory workers retain a working-class life-style.

In his analysis of affluent automobile assembly workers, Berger concluded that even suburban residence did not produce middle-class behavior in his blue-collar workers. Mackenzie is forceful in rejecting the hypothesis that American society is becoming homogenized. He writes that hypotheses relating to the merger of the blue-collar elite and the white-collar middle-class "are simply inaccurate. . . . There exists in the middle ranges of the American class structure an aristocracy of skilled labor, isolated both from the working class and from the lower reaches of the established middle-class."[3]

We would agree with Gans that it is a serious error for social planners and other interventionists to assume that middle-class values are now accepted by most Americans. The West Enders studied by Gans did not even define their neighborhood as a slum, yet it was condemned by urban renewal specialists and slated for demolition. After living in the area for several months Gans concluded that the neighborhood was not a slum, and he agreed with the residents that it should not be demolished.

After some five years of participating in the life of The Oasis I came away with the conclusion that many of the blue-collar workers at the tavern (excluding the alcoholics and some of the divorced persons) have a more spontaneous, less competitive life than a great many middle-class strivers known to me. Given steady employment, it is hard to beat the life of a skilled construction worker.

During the period of this study one of my sons, a university student, obtained a summer job helping a man build a house. In the process my son had a chance to see the home take shape from the pouring of the concrete for the basement to the final landscaping. When the summer was over and the house ready for a family to move in, my son reported that he never had had such satisfaction in anything he had done so far in his life. He drove his mother and me out to see the house when it was completed; it was the first tangible accomplishment in his middle-class life that he could point to. How many white collar workers ever have such job satisfaction?

It is interesting that in over two hundred tape recorded interviews with Americans (both male and female) about their jobs, Studs Terkel concluded that one of the persons who enjoyed his work most was a stone-mason.[4]

SOCIAL CLASS SUSPICION AND DISTRUST

Looking back at my five years at The Oasis I find myself somewhat surprised at the depth and extent of the suspicion and distrust the blue-collar workers have of the white-collar middle and upper classes. This has already been discussed and needs only to be underlined here.

In a democratic society there are very real problems when one segment of the society does not respect or trust another segment. All of America's leaders are white-collar: economic, political, religious, even labor leaders become white-collar as they ascend the union ladder. Who, then, can win and retain the respect and loyalty of the blue-collar elite?

As the blue-collar worker looks around he sees more and more white-collar people, not only in his community but also in positions of power. Like the farmer, he begins to feel isolated and forgotten. Almost all of the television programs feature white-collar people (unless you consider Archie Bunker blue-collar); the movies feature white-collar men and women; mass magazines deal largely with the middle class; and advertisements are overwhelmingly white-collar. Thus the blue-collar worker scarcely ever sees himself portrayed in the society. His wife does not experience quite the same feeling of exclusion because she identifies more with the white-collar world.

This distrust is not entirely one-sided; many white-collar persons have similar feelings toward the blue-collar workers. A retail salesman who frequents The Oasis made this comment: "The dumb bastards voted in Nixon and now they are crying in their beer. What in the hell did they think the Republicans would do when they got control of the federal government? All these guys care about is higher wages and more fringe benefits—they don't care about the rest of us."

When a national news story was written about this book, a white-collar worker in New England wrote to me about my statement that the construction workers seem to enjoy their work: "It's not the tangible things these fellows leave behind that makes them happy," he wrote, "rather, it's an intangible—the prospect of unending repair work at exorbitant rates, thanks to their sloppy workmanship." One can feel the hostility and contempt in this letter that millions of white-collar people must feel toward the blue-collar aristocrats.

There seems to be no immediate solution to this interclass hostility and suspicion in American society; a leader would have to emerge who could win support and loyalty from different levels of the social class system. Dwight Eisenhower was apparently such a person but nobody at the moment seems to have this kind of appeal.

POLITICS

As the Watergate investigation proceeded, and after the scandal about Vice President Agnew, the men at The Oasis sank into an even gloomier mood about politics in America. These national developments were augmented by the revelation that many small town officials in the state had been accepting pay-offs from chemical companies for purchasing city supplies from favored firms. Until this point most of the men at the tavern had felt that local politics was relatively clean (they trusted the village mayor, for example), but now their disillusionment was complete.

Actually, many of the regulars at The Oasis were not especially disturbed by the Watergate affair because these men have always believed most politicians to be "crooked." What really angered the men at the tavern about Nixon was his so-called wage and price control program. One carpenter said: "The sonofabitch promised us he would control prices and profits if we would limit our wage demands. So we get 5 percent a year while prices go up 15 percent and the big companies make a killing. That is real horseshit to me."

With Nixon and the Republicans out of favor, who will the men turn to in the 1976 presidential election? As of 1974 one could make the following guesses:

1. Gerald Ford might do fairly well with these men if he runs for the White House in 1976. The men do not blame Ford for Watergate, and they think "the sonofabitch is honest."* As was indicated earlier in the book, the men at The Oasis rank honesty first in public officials—above intelligence, for example. Ford has some of the homespun qualities of Harry Truman and Dwight Eisenhower, both of whom are well thought of by the construction workers at the tavern.

2. George Wallace may have lost his appeal for these men.[5] The campus riots and the militant black movement, forces which drove these men toward Wallace in 1968 and 1972, are less visible now. Furthermore, these men seem to doubt that the disabled Wallace has the drive he once had. One man said: "Once you get shot like that you're never the same again." It needs to be remembered, however, that another man in a wheelchair, Franklin D. Roosevelt, enjoyed great popularity with blue-collar workers in the 1930s and the 1940s.

3. George McGovern has never had any deep rapport with these men. He is too "left" for them—they dislike, for example, his support of amnesty for the men who refused to serve in Vietnam. The workers at The Oasis also regard McGovern as a "smooth talker"—a person they automatically distrust.

4. Ted Kennedy—what would his chances be with these men if he ran? As much experience as these workers have had with liquor, they tend to believe that Kennedy was drunk the night the girl drowned in his car on Cape Cod. And as much experience as they have had with sex, most of the men at the tavern are not convinced that Kennedy was not involved in some way with the girl. At the same time, however, as men of the world, these workers can understand such things and might eventually have supported Kennedy if he had run for the White House. One reason is that they have relatively little choice at the moment; the other possibilities seem even worse.

It should be remembered that the men at The Oasis do not vote *for* somebody, they vote *against* somebody. That is their stance toward life in general, not just politics.

5. Of the men in the national news these days Senator Howard

---

*This was written before the Ford pardon of Nixon.

Baker seems to have made a good impression on many of the men at the tavern. Baker strikes them as a humble man—a quality they tend to admire in public figures. Baker also does not impress them as a "smooth talker," a quality they do not like in their politicians. It could be that Baker would do well with the blue-collar workers at The Oasis.

FUTURE SHOCK

No matter what social problem is being discussed (except that of conservation and protection of the natural environment) the reaction of these blue-collar aristocrats goes through the following cycle:

1. The problem doesn't exist. Women, or blacks, or the poor are better off today than they used to be, a lot better. So what are they bitching about?
2. The whole fuss has been stirred up by a few radicals. There's no real problem, only somebody "shooting off his big mouth."
3. If you think it's bad here you should see it someplace else— Italy, for example.
4. Why don't the people who don't like it here go back where they came from? The men admit that this is no solution to "the woman problem" but they think it would work for some other problems. "Why don't the blacks go back to Africa if they don't like it here?" one man said.
5. To hell with it, let's have another drink.

These men refuse to face the problems of the contemporary world except the ones related to the preservation of the natural environment. They would like for the world to be like it was when they were growing up; a majority of them spent their youth on family farms, or in small rural villages,[6] and their memories are of peace and quiet and satisfaction with things as they were. World War II was a violent interlude for most of these men, and after the war they wanted merely to resume life as it had been before. Nothing about the contemporary world (except the higher wages) seems as good as what they knew in their youth.

Some of these men are not even sure they would like the four-day week being proposed for American industry. "I think the guys would drink too much if they had another day off," a carpenter said. "Look how bad it is now on weekends—it would be just that much worse."

Are these men atypical in their view of the contemporary scene? In his widely read book, *Future Shock*, Alvin Toffler argues that most of us are confused, dismayed, and frightened by the problems confronting the modern world.[7] Some of these, such as the pollution of the environment, are so new that man's experience offers no guidelines for action. The village mayor made this comment to me: "Sure I'm against pollution of the environment—but what do I do about it? The state and the federal government have not issued any standards or any model legislation. I don't know what action to take."

It may well be that the blue-collar elite are no more confused than the rest of us, only more blunt in their comments.

AULD LANG SYNE

My last official visit to The Oasis (1974) turned out to be a historic occasion: our pool team, of which I was a member, won the league championship that night in the final match of the season; a player on the visiting team had become the proud father of a son that afternoon; and our coach (an honorific title) was treating his "boys"* to what seemed like an endless round of drinks.

As the evening developed the tavern became an amiable scene of happy chaos, reminding me of prints of English tavern life in the eighteenth century. Men were dancing together when they couldn't find a woman to dance with; the women were in such great demand as dancing partners they scarcely had time to go to the powder room; in one corner of the tavern two men were on the floor in a friendly wrestling match; the happy (and somewhat drunk) new father was passing out cigars to the women as well as the men; and at the bar an attractive young divorcee was fending off passes from all directions (she told me later that one man had even proposed

---

*Why do coaches always refer to grown men (or even overgrown men) as "boys"?

marriage). A pool player on the visiting team became confused and used the seven ball as the cue ball as he executed an otherwise brilliant shot (his buddies had to point out that the cue ball is the white ball whereas the seven ball is not white, that using the seven ball as the cue ball constitutes a foul, and that therefore it was not his turn to shoot again even though he had sunk his object ball), all of which only seemed to confuse the player even more until his friends suggested he go back to the bar for another drink and all would be well.

When it became clear that The Oasis team would win not only the match that night but also the league championship, the tavern owner became elated (some people would say confused) and began buying drinks for everybody—a custom he usually reserves for New Year's Eve and St. Patrick's Day.

I remember being kissed by our "cheerleader" (the attractive wife of one of our players) when my partner and I won our last game of the match. The balance of the evening is somewhat hazy but I remember distinctly that there were no fights—unusual for such a night at The Oasis. Fortunately, I was not driving and walked home alone.

By winning the championship our pool team won the league jackpot of approximately $300 which was to be used for a big party later on for players and their wives—all the steak you could eat and all the beer and liquor you could drink. That would be quite an evening.

Notes

Introduction

1. Elliot Liebow, *Tally's Corner* (Boston: Little, Brown and Co., 1967).
2. Herbert J. Gans, *The Urban Villagers* (New York: The Free Press, 1962). See also Gan's study, *The Levittowners* (New York: Random House, 1967). Gans utilized the participant-observation research method in both of these studies.
3. William Foote Whyte, *Street Corner Society* rev. ed. (Chicago: University of Chicago Press, 1955).
4. W. Fred Cottrell, *The Railroader* (Palo Alto, Calif.: Stanford University Press, 1940).
5. See, for example, Arnold W. Green, "The Middle Class Male Child and Neurosis," *American Sociological Review* II (1946): 31-41.
6. For an illustration of Erving Goffman's work, see his *Asylums* (New York: Doubleday & Co., 1961).
7. Joseph T. Howell, *Hard Living on Clay Street* (New York: Anchor Books, 1973).
8. See John H. Goldthorpe et al., *The Affluent Worker in the Class Structure* (New York: Cambridge University Press, 1969).
9. See Goffman, *Asylums*.
10. Howell, *Hard Living*.
11. Liebow, *Tally's Corner*.
12. For an interesting participant-observation study of pool halls and pool hustlers, see Ned Polsky, *Hustlers, Beats, and Others* (Chicago: Aldine Publishing Co., 1967).
13. In his 1955 edition of *Street Corner Society* Whyte has an extensive discussion of the problems in participant-observation research. See pp. 279-358.

205

14. Alfred C. Kinsey et al., *Sexual Behavior in the Human Male* (Philadelphia: W. B. Saunders, 1948).
15. Some of the research problems of social anthropologists are discussed in Clyde Kluckhohn, *Mirror for Man* (New York: McGraw-Hill, 1949).
16. See Reo G. Fortune, *Sorcerers of Dobu* (New York: E. P. Dutton, 1932). Fortune reported the Dobuans to be extremely paranoid in their view of the world, but my student, who had lived in Dobu for a year during World War II, did not have this impression of the society.
17. Persons interested in participant-observation research might wish to examine additional studies utilizing this method. In addition to the publications cited earlier the following are recommended: Gerald D. Suttles, *The Social Order of the Slum* (Chicago: University of Chicago Press, 1968); Laud Humphreys, *Tearoom Trade* (Chicago: Aldine Publishing Co., 1970); Sherri Cavan, *Liquor License* (Chicago: Aldine Publishing Co., 1966).

Chapter 1: The Tavern, the Town, and the Professor

1. For an interesting analysis of different types of bars, see Sherri Cavan's *Liquor License* (Chicago: Aldine Publishing Co., 1966).
2. On some of the problems of suburban communities similar to Lakeside, see Robert Wood, *Suburbia: Its People and Their Politics* (Boston: Houghton Mifflin, 1958); and Charles M. Haar, ed., *The End of Innocence: A Suburban Reader* (Glenview) Ill: Scott, Foresman, 1972).
3. James Boswell, *The Life of Samuel Johnson* (New York: The Modern Library, 1970), p. 592.

Chapter 2: The World of Work

1. The function of the job in establishing a man's self-image and his position in the community was graphically illustrated by studies of unemployed men in America in the 1930s. See, for example, Ruth Cavan and Katherine Ranck, *The Family and the Depression* (Chicago: University of Chicago Press, 1938); and Mirra

Komarovsky, *The Unemployed Man and his Family* (New York: Dryden Press, 1940).

2. See Charles A. Reich, *The Greening of America* (New York: Random House, 1970); and Keith Melville, *Communes in the Counter Culture* (New York: William Morrow, 1972).

3. In the 1960s the United Automobile Workers bargained for early retirement because of the monotony and repetitive nature of the work on the assembly line.

4. This is the theme of the Reich study cited above. When it was published, this book was on the national best-seller lists for approximately a year.

5. Francis Russell, *The Shadow of Blooming Grove: Warren G. Harding in His Times* (New York: McGraw-Hill, 1968).

6. The electrician's union in New York City has had a thirty-hour week for the last decade. This means that overtime pay begins when thirty hours are completed.

7. Reich, *Greening of America*, p. 243.

8. For a discussion of the farm background of blue-collar workers, see Arthur B. Shostak, *Blue Collar Life* (New York: Random House, 1969).

9. For a general analysis of vertical mobility in American Society, see Theodore Caplow, *The Sociology of Work* (New York: McGraw-Hill, 1964), pp. 59-81.

10. For a discussion of blue-collar workers who have become operators of small businesses, see Ivar Berg and David Rogers, "Former Blue-Collarites in Small Business," in *Blue-Collar World*, ed. Arthur B. Shostak and William Gomberg (Englewood Cliffs, N.J.: Prentice-Hall, 1964), pp. 558-574.

11. Bennett M. Berger, *Working-Class Suburb* (Berkeley, Calif.: University of California Press, 1960); John H. Goldthorpe et al., *The Affluent Worker in the Class Structure* (New York: Cambridge University Press, 1969).

12. See David O. Arnold, ed., *The Sociology of Subcultures* (Berkeley, Calif.: The Glendessary Press, 1970).

13. Goldthorpe et al., *Affluent Worker in the Class Structure*.

14. For a general discussion of trade unions in American society, see Caplow, *Sociology of Work*, pp. 191-213.

15. John H. Goldthorpe et al., *The Affluent Worker: Industrial Attitudes and Behavior* (New York: Cambridge University Press, 1968).

Chapter 3: Marriage

1. See Mirra Komarovsky, *Blue-Collar Marriage* (New York: Random House, 1962); Herbert J. Gans, *The Urban Villagers* (New York: The Free Press, 1962); and Arthur B. Shostak, *Blue-Collar Life* (New York: Random House, 1969).

2. For a similar view of marriage in our society, see Jessie Bernard, *The Future of Marriage* (New York: World Publishing Co., 1972).

3. Bernard, *Future of Marriage*.

4. John H. Goldthorpe et al., *The Affluent Worker in the Class Structure* (New York: Cambridge University Press, 1969), p. 108.

5. In addition to Komarovsky, *Blue-Collar Marriage,* and Gans, *Urban Villagers,* see also Patricia Cayo Sexton, "Wife of the 'Happy' Worker," in *Blue-Collar World,* ed. Arthur B. Shostak and William Gomberg (Englewood Cliffs, N.J.: Prentice-Hall, 1964), pp. 81-85.

6. Gans, *Urban Villagers,* chap. 3.

7. In addition to the sources cited earlier, see also Nathan Hurvitz, "Marital Strain in the Blue-Collar Family," in *Blue-Collar World,* ed. Shostak and Gomberg, pp. 92-109; and Irving Tallman, 'Working-Class Wives: Fulfillment or Crisis?," *Journal of Marriage and the Family* 31 (February 1969): 65-72.

8. Ernest Barth and Walter Watson, "Social Stratification and Family in Mass Society," *Social Forces* 45 (1966-1967): 97-108.

9. In one of the earliest studies of social class in America the Lynds pointed out this difference between blue-collar and white-collar work. See Robert S. Lynd and Helen Lynd, *Middletown* (New York: Harcourt, Brace & Co., 1929).

10. Ernest Burgess and Paul Wallin, *Engagement and Marriage* (Philadelphia, Pa.: J. B. Lippincott Co., 1953).

11. For the history of divorce in America since the nineteenth century, see William O'Neill, *Divorce in the Progressive Era* (New Haven, Conn.: Yale University Press, 1967).

12. John Cuber and Peggy Haroff, *The Significant Americans* (New York: Appleton-Century, 1965). See also E. E. LeMasters, "Holy Deadlock: A Study of Unsuccessful Marriages," *Sociological Quarterly* 21 (1959): 86-91.

Chapter 4: Marital Failure

1. William J. Goode, *After Divorce* (New York: The Free Press, 1956).
2. See Morton M. Hunt, *The World of the Formerly Married* (New York: McGraw-Hill Book Co., 1966).
3. See Goode, *After Divorce;* and Hunt, *World of the Formerly Married.*
4. The failure of divorced men to make support payments has become a national problem. The situation was reviewed in *The Milwaukee Journal,* July 7, 1972, p. 18. In Milwaukee County alone, as of the above date, over six million dollars in delinquent support payments were known to the Domestic Relations Court.
5. In an interesting study of divorced men and women John O'Brien refers to facade marriages as being "depleted"—they are no longer vital. See his *The Decision to Divorce* (Ph.D. diss., University of Wisconsin, 1971).
6. For a more detailed analysis of facade marriage, see E. E. LeMasters, "The Middle Aged Man and His Marriage," in *The Middle Aged Man in Contemporary Society* (London: Berkeley Publishers, 1972). John Cuber and Peggy Haroff have an extensive analysis of facade marriages in their study, *The Significant Americans* (New York: Appleton-Century, 1965).
7. An excellent discussion of the concept of "successful divorce" will be found in Mel Krantzler, *Creative Divorce* (New York: Evans Publishing Co., 1974).

Chapter 5: Battle of the Sexes

1. For a general analysis of the male-female relationship in human society, see Margaret Mead, *Male and Female* (New York: William Morrow & Co., 1949).
2. Lee Rainwater, *And the Poor Get Children* (Chicago: Quadrangle Books, 1960), p. 77.
3. For a scholarly analysis of how men have dominated Western society, see Charles W. Ferguson, *The Male Attitude* (Boston: Little, Brown & Co., 1966). For the feminine version, see Elaine

Kendall, *The Upper Hand* (Boston: Little, Brown & Co., 1965).

4. See Orville G. Brim, Jr., *Education for Child Rearing* (New York: Russell Sage Foundation, 1959).

5. In a very controversial book, Lionel Tiger has argued that men tend to seek male companionship because male bonding was crucial for human survival in man's early history. See his analysis, *Men in Groups* (New York: Random House, 1969). For some interesting and provocative replies to Tiger and the men who agree with him, see Michele Hoffnung Garskof, ed., *Roles Women Play: Readings toward Women's Liberation* (Belmont, Calif.: Brooks/Cole Publishing Company, 1971).

6. Mead, *Male and Female.*

7. For an excellent historical analysis of the feminist movement in the United States, see William L. O'Neill, *Everyone Was Brave: The Rise and Fall of Feminism in America* (Chicago: Quadrangle Books, 1969).

8. David Riesman et al., *The Lonely Crowd* (New Haven, Conn.: Yale University Press, 1961).

Chapter 6: The Sexual Way of Life

1. See Alfred C. Kinsey et al., *Sexual Behavior in the Human Male* (Philadelphia: W. B. Saunders Co, 1946).

2. William Foote Whyte, "A Slum Sex Code," *American Journal of Sociology* 49 (1943): 24-31.

3. Kinsey, *Male Sexual Behavior,* chap. 10.

4. See Luigi Barzini, *The Italians* (New York: Atheneum Press, 1964).

5. Kinsey, *Male Sexual Behavior,* pp. 321-326.

6. For a study of divorced persons and their sexual patterns, see Morton Hunt, *The World of the Formerly Married* (New York: McGraw-Hill Book Co., 1966).

7. Ibid.

8. For an analysis of sexual behavior in bars, see Sherri Cavan, *Liquor License: An Ethnography of Bar Behavior* (Chicago: Aldine Publishing Co, 1966).

9. For a general analysis of adultery in American society see Mor-

ton Hunt, *The Affair* (New York: World Publishing Co., 1969); and Gerhard Neubeck, ed., *Extramarital Relations* (Englewood Cliffs, N.J.: Prentice-Hall, 1969).

10. For an analysis of "opening moves" at bars, see Cavan, *Liquor License*, pp. 181-190.

11. Similar patterns have been reported for tigers, lions, and the large apes. See George Schaller, *The Mountain Gorilla* (Chicago: University of Chicago Press, 1963).

12. For a discussion of the homosexual in our society, see Laud Humphreys, *Out of the Closets* (Englewood Cliffs, N.J.: Prentice-Hall, 1972).

13. Almost any introduction to Freudian theory will summarize his theory of homosexuality.

Chapter 7: Children and Kinfolk

1. Excellent summaries of social class subcultures in American society will be found in: Herbert J. Gans, *The Urban Villagers* (New York: The Free Press, 1962); Robin M. Williams, Jr., *American Society*, 3d ed. (New York: Alfred A. Knopf, 1970); and Max Lerner, *America as a Civilization* (New York: Simon & Schuster, 1957).

2. David Riesman et al., *The Lonely Crowd*, rev. ed. (New Haven: Yale University Press, 1961).

3. Daniel Miller and Guy Swanson, *The Changing American Parent* (New York: John Wiley & Sons, 1958).

4. Donald G. McKinley, *Social Class and Family Life* (New York: The Free Press, 1964).

5. For a discussion of upper-class child rearing systems, see E. E. LeMasters, *Parents in Modern America*, 2d ed. (Homewood, Ill.: The Dorsey Press, 1974), chap. 5.

6. An analysis of parental models will be found in Evelyn Duvall, "Conceptions of Parenthood," *American Journal of Sociology* 52 (1946): 193-203; and Mirra Komarovsky, *Blue-Collar Marriage* (New York: Random House, 1964), pp. 73-81.

7. For an analysis of parental models in our society, see LeMasters, *Parents in Modern America*, chap. 12.

8. An extensive analysis of the anxiety and guilt felt by many American parents will be found in LeMasters, *Parents in Modern America.*

9. See Elliot Liebow, *Talley's Corner* (Boston: Little, Brown & Co., 1967).

10. Miller and Swanson, *Changing American Parent.*

11. For an analysis of these trends see George Meany, *Labor Looks at Capitalism,* Publication no. 139 (Washington, D.C.: AFL-CIO, 1966).

12. See Orville G. Brim, Jr., *Education for Child Rearing* (New York: Russell Sage Foundation, 1959).

13. For an interesting study of the grandparent role in American society, see Joan F. Robertson, "Grandparenthood: A Study of Role Conceptions of Grandmothers" (Ph.D. diss., School of Social Work, University of Wisconsin, 1971).

14. For an extensive review of the research on kinship in the 1960s, see Bert Adams, "Isolation, Function, and Beyond: American Kinship in the 1960's," *Journal of Marriage and the Family* 32 (1970): 575-597. Gans has an analysis of kinship ties in his study of blue-collar workers in Boston in *The Urban Villagers.* In *Blue-Collar Marriage* Mirra Komarovsky has a discussion of kinship (chapter 11). See also Eugene Litwak, "Extended Kin Relations in an Industrial Society," in *Social Structure and the Family,* ed. Ethel Shanas and Gordon Streib (Englewood Cliffs, N.J.: Prentice-Hall, 1965), pp. 290-323.

15. For an analysis of social class continuity and sibling relationships, see E. E. LeMasters, "Social Class Mobility and Family Integration," *Marriage and Family Living* 16 (1954): 226-232.

16. See Murray Hausknecht, "The Blue-Collar Joiner," in *Blue-Collar World,* ed. by Arthur B. Shostak and William Gomberg (Engelwood Cliffs, N.J.: Prentice-Hall, 1964), pp. 207-215.

17. For discussions of ethnic factors in American society, see Williams, *American Society;* and Lerner, *America as a Civilization.*

Chapter 8: Tavern Social Life

1. See Herbert J. Gans, *The Urban Villagers* (New York: The Free Press, 1962), pp. 28-31, for an analysis of blue-collar "action seekers."

2. William Foote Whyte, *Street Corner Society*, rev. ed. (Chicago: University of Chicago Press, 1955).

3. For a useful analysis of gambling in Western society, see Robert D. Herman, ed., *Gambling* (New York: Harper & Row, 1967).

4. For some interesting observations of pool hustlers in more elaborate establishments than The Oasis, see Ned Polsky, *Hustlers, Beats, and Others* (Chicago: Aldine Publishing Co., 1967).

5. The English are even more compulsive than Americans in their pursuit of gambling. See Goeffrey Gorer, "British Life—It's A Gamble," *New York Times Magazine*, September 1, 1963. Reprinted in Herman, ed., *Gambling*, pp. 80-87.

6. Whyte, *Street Corner Society*.

7. For a discussion of the way in which gambling reduces the monotony of life, see the analysis of "policy numbers" by St. Clair Drake and Horace Cayton in Herman, ed., *Gambling*, pp. 3-10.

8. This is the major theme of David Riesman et al., *The Lonely Crowd*, rev. ed., (New Haven: Yale University Press, 1961).

9. *Webster's New World Dictionary of the American Language* (Cleveland: World Publishing Co., 1957), p. 277.

Chapter 9: Drinking Patterns at the Tavern

1. For an attempt to define alcoholism, see Harrison Trice, *Alcoholism in America* (New York: McGraw-Hill Book Co., 1966), pp. 28-41.

2. Ibid., pp. 48-49.

3. See ibid., pp. 62-68, for some of the strategies used by wives to cope with their husband's drinking.

4. For an analysis of alcoholism as a major public health problem in the United States, see American Psychiatric Association and the National Association for Mental Health, *The Treatment of Alcoholism* (Washington, D.C.: The Associations, 1967); and U.S. Department of Health, Education, and Welfare, *Alcohol and Alcoholism* (Washington, D.C.: The Department, 1968).

5. State of Wisconsin, Department of Motor Vehicles, *Annual Report* (Madison, Wis.: The Department, 1965).

6. In an interesting study David Gottlieb discovered that taverns

tolerate much more disruptive behavior from their regular customers than they do from transients. See his paper, "The Neighborhood Tavern and the Cocktail Lounge: A Study of Class
Differences," *American Journal of Sociology* 62 (May 1957):
550-562.
7. *Milwaukee Journal,* April 2, 1970, p. 22.
8. Ibid.
9. The writer is indebted to Robert Mohelnitzky, for use of material from his paper, "The Neighborhood Tavern," submitted for
a graduate seminar, "Problems of the Contemporary American
Family," School of Social Work, University of Wisconsin, Madison, Wis., 1970.

Chapter 10: Politics, Race, and Religion

1. See John H. Goldthorpe et al., *The Affluent Worker: Political
Attitudes and Behavior* (New York: Cambridge University Press,
1968).
2. Arthur Kornhauser, Albert Mayer, and Harold Sheppard, *When
Labor Votes* (New York: University Books, 1956); Bennett M.
Berger, *Working-Class Suburb* (Berkeley, Calif.: University of
California Press, 1960).
3. An interesting account of the liberal era in Wisconsin under the
Progressives will be found in John R. Commons, *Myself* (Madison, Wis.: University of Wisconsin Press, 1963).
4. In 1971 the Department of Defense announced that 1,144 men
from Wisconsin had been killed in Vietnam. See *Wisconsin State
Journal,* July 3, 1971, p. 1.
5. Michael Harrington, *The Other America* (New York: The Mac-
millan Co., 1963).
6. For the attack on students in New York City by a group of
"hard hats," see John Brooks, *The Go-Go Years* (New York:
Weybright and Talley, 1973), pp. 6-10.
7. Some studies of the Kent State tragedy conclude that the students *did* disperse when ordered to by the national guard. See,
for example, the report of the United Methodist Church, written
by Peter Davies, *The Truth about Kent State* (New York: Farrar,
Straus, & Giroux), 1973.
8. For a valuable history of the feminist movement in the United

States, see William L. O'Neill, *Everyone Was Brave: The Rise and Fall of Feminism in America* (Chicago: Quadrangle Books, 1969).

9. For a comparison of racial attitudes and those toward women, see Caroline Bird, *Born Female* (New York: Pocket Books, 1971), chap. 6.

10. Various observers have commented on the fatalistic attitude of blue-collar groups. See, for example, Herbert J. Gans, *The Urban Villagers* (New York: The Free Press, 1962).

11. See, for example, Lewis S. Feuer, *The Conflict of Generations* (New York: Basic Books, 1969).

Chapter 11: Reflections on The Oasis

1. See Herbert J. Gans, *The Urban Villagers* (New York: The Free Press, 1962); Bennett M. Berger, *Working-Class Suburb* (Berkeley, Calif.: University of California Press, 1968); Mirra Komarovsky, *Blue-Collar Marriage* (New York: Random House, 1962); Gavin Mackenzie, *The Aristocracy of Labor* (New York: Cambridge University Press, 1974); John H. Goldthorpe et al., *The Affluent Worker: Industrial Attitudes and Behavior* (New York: Cambridge University Press, 1968), *The Affluent Worker: Political Attitudes and Behavior* (New York: Cambridge University Press, 1968), and *The Affluent Worker in the Class Structure* (New York: Cambridge University Press, 1969).

2. Gans, *Urban Villagers*, p. x.

3. Mackenzie, *Aristocracy of Labor*, p. 162. Unfortunately, this excellent study did not become available until this manuscript was in its final stages.

4. See Studs Terkel, *Working* (New York: Pantheon Books, 1974).

5. Some studies have concluded that Wallace appealed almost as much to white-collar workers as he did to blue-collar persons. See, for example, Richard Hamilton, "Liberal Intelligentsia and White Backlash," in *The World of the Blue-Collar Worker*, ed. Irving Howe (New York: Quadrangle Books, 1972).

6. For a discussion of the rural background of blue-collar workers, see Arthur B. Shostak, *Blue-Collar Life* (New York: Random House, 1969).

7. Alvin Toffler, *Future Shock* (New York: Random House, 1970).

Index